Spies in Space
Reflections on National Reconnaissance and the Manned Orbiting Laboratory

Courtney V.K. Homer

Nimble Books LLC: The AI Lab for Book-Lovers
~ Fred Zimmerman, Editor ~

Humans and AI making books richer, more diverse, and more surprising.

Publishing Information

(c) 2023 Nimble Books LLC
ISBN: 978-1-60888-265-6

AI-generated Keyword Phrases

Manned Orbiting Laboratory program; United States Air Force; military reconnaissance; Cold War; program cancellation; cost concerns; international relations; role of humans in space; training program; crew members; MOL system development; personal accounts; program termination; consequences of cancellation; layoffs; transfer to NASA; complexities; controversies.

Cover Art

A 1960 concept image of the United States Air Force's proposed Manned Orbiting Laboratory (MOL) that was intended to test the military usefulness of having humans in orbit. The station's baseline configuration was that of a two-person Gemini B spacecraft that could be attached to a laboratory vehicle. The structure was planned to launch onboard a Titan IIIC rocket. The station would be used for a month and then the astronauts could return to the Gemini capsule for transport back to Earth. The first launch of the MOL was scheduled for December 15, 1969, but was then pushed back to the fall of 1971. The program was cancelled by Defense Secretary Melvin R. Laird in 1969 after the estimated cost of the program had risen in excess of billion, and had already spent .3 billion. Some of the military astronauts selected for the program then transferred to NASA and became some of the first people to fly the Space Shuttle, including Richard Truly, who later became the NASA Administrator.

Publisher's Note

In the world of deeply classified military projects, "never-weres" and "might have beens" can shed great light on what actually has been happening behind the scenes. The Manned Orbital Laboratory, a secret project that was cancelled in 1969, illustrates that for more than sixty years, the US government has been energetically seeking persistent, easily-retasked, adaptive, and above all intelligent capabilities for monitoring adversaries from space. For those interested in military space[1], the history offers an essential reference point. If the MOL had flown, it would have been super cool; but the US secured the desired capabilities by other means, many of which are still deep black.

---

[1] Indeed, *"For All Mankind."* —Ed.

ANNOTATIONS

- Publishing Information ii
- AI-generated Keyword Phrases ii
- Cover Art ii
- Publisher's Note iv
- Abstracts vi
  - TL;DR (one word) vi
  - Explain It To Me Like I'm Five Years Old vi
  - TL;DR (vanilla) vi
  - Scientific Style vii
  - Action Items vii
- Viewpoints viii
  - Grounds for Dissent viii
  - Red Team Critique ix
  - MAGA Perspective xi
- Page-by-Page Summaries xiii
- Notable Passages xxi

Abstracts

TL;DR (one word)

Space spies.[2]

Explain It To Me Like I'm Five Years Old

The Manned Orbiting Laboratory (MOL) was a program developed by the United States Air Force in the 1960s. They wanted to create a special space station that people could live in and use for spying on other countries during the Cold War. This program had many goals and faced a lot of challenges, but unfortunately, it was eventually canceled. People had different opinions about MOL, some thought it was too expensive and could cause problems with other countries, while others believed it was important. Either way, it never happened.

TL;DR (vanilla)

The document provides an overview of the Manned Orbiting Laboratory (MOL) program developed by the US Air Force in the 1960s for military reconnaissance. It discusses objectives, challenges, and cancellation, highlighting debates and concerns. It also mentions crew training, roles, and system development. Personal accounts express disappointment over termination and mention consequences like layoffs and transfer to NASA. Overall, it provides insights into the complexities and controversies of the MOL program.

---

[2] This is a human override of the AI original, which was "MOL program". Sometimes computers are boring. —Ed.

SCIENTIFIC STYLE

This document provides a comprehensive overview of the Manned Orbiting Laboratory (MOL) program, a United States Air Force initiative in the 1960s aimed at developing a manned space platform for military reconnaissance during the Cold War. The document explores the objectives, challenges, and eventual cancellation of the program, as well as the debates and differing opinions surrounding MOL. It discusses concerns about cost, international relations, and the role of humans in space. The document also covers the training program for MOL crew members, their roles and responsibilities, and the development of the MOL system. Personal accounts express shock and disappointment over the program's termination, and mention the consequences such as layoffs and the transfer of MOL crew members to NASA. Overall, this document offers insights into the complexities and controversies surrounding the MOL program.

ACTION ITEMS

Further research the MOL program to gain a deeper understanding of its historical context and significance.

Analyze the debates and differing opinions surrounding MOL to assess the various factors that contributed to its cancellation.

Explore the impact of the MOL program's cancellation on the individuals involved and the broader space industry.

Consider the lessons learned from the MOL program and how they can be applied to current and future space exploration initiatives.

Viewpoints

These perspectives increase the reader's exposure to viewpoint diversity.

Grounds for Dissent

A member of the organization responsible for this document might have principled, substantive reasons to dissent from this report due to the following:

Ethical Concerns: One of the dissenting views could stem from ethical concerns regarding the purpose of the Manned Orbiting Laboratory program. Some individuals within the organization might argue that the program's primary objective of military reconnaissance is contrary to ethical principles, as it involves potentially infringing upon the privacy and sovereignty of other nations. These dissenters may believe that the use of space exploration for military purposes goes against the spirit of exploration and peaceful cooperation.

Cost Inefficiency: Another principled reason for dissent could be the belief that the MOL program was an exorbitant and wasteful use of resources. Dissenting members might argue that the funds allocated for the program could have been better utilized in addressing pressing domestic issues or invested in scientific research and development with broader societal benefits. They may contend that the program's cancellation was a necessary step to prevent further unnecessary expenditure.

Technological Limitations: Some dissenting members might voice substantive concerns about the feasibility and effectiveness of the MOL program. They may argue that the technological capabilities of the era were not advanced enough to support sustained manned space missions for military purposes. These dissenters might present arguments based on scientific evidence or expert opinions indicating that unmanned satellites or other alternative methods would have been more efficient and cost-effective for reconnaissance purposes.

International Relations: Dissent could also arise from individuals within the organization who hold strong beliefs in promoting international cooperation and peace. They might argue that the MOL program, being a military endeavor developed during the height of the Cold War, contributed to the escalation of tensions between the United States and the Soviet Union. These dissenters could contend that such programs hindered efforts for disarmament and trust-building between nations, thus undermining global security and stability.

Human Risk: Dissenters might raise concerns about the risks associated with sending humans into space for military purposes. They may argue that manned missions increase the potential for casualties and loss of life, which could be avoided by relying on unmanned systems. These members might prioritize the safety of human lives over the potential benefits gained through manned missions and advocate for alternative approaches to achieve the same objectives.

In summary, a principled dissent from this report could arise due to ethical concerns regarding the program's purpose, cost inefficiency, technological limitations, negative impact on international relations, and the risks associated with manned missions. These dissenting views reflect a sincere commitment to principles, values, and the pursuit of alternatives that align better with their vision of progress and global cooperation.

RED TEAM CRITIQUE

Upon reviewing the document providing an overview of the Manned Orbiting Laboratory (MOL) program, several points of critique arise.

Firstly, while the document does provide a comprehensive overview of the objectives, challenges, and cancellation of the MOL program, it lacks a critical analysis of the feasibility and effectiveness of the program's goals. It would be beneficial to include an evaluation of whether the program's intended military reconnaissance purposes were attainable and if the MOL system was likely to succeed in meeting these objectives. Without such analysis, the document may present a biased perspective that fails to address potential shortcomings and limitations.

Additionally, the document mentions debates and differing opinions surrounding the MOL program, but it fails to provide a balanced representation of these debates. It primarily focuses on concerns about cost, international relations, and the role of humans in space without adequately addressing potential counterarguments or alternative viewpoints. A more robust analysis of the arguments on both sides of these debates would better equip readers with a comprehensive understanding of the controversies surrounding the program.

Moreover, while the personal accounts of individuals involved in the program do add a human element to the document, they appear to be overwhelmingly one-sided in expressing shock and disappointment over the termination of MOL. It is essential to include a range of perspectives, including those who may have supported the program's cancellation or had reservations about its efficacy. This would help present a more balanced view of the consequences and implications of ending the program.

Furthermore, the document briefly mentions the training program for MOL crew members, their roles, and responsibilities, but fails to delve into specific details or provide an in-depth analysis of these aspects. A more detailed examination of the training program and crew member responsibilities would contribute to a more comprehensive understanding of the challenges faced by the MOL program.

Finally, the document mentions the consequences of the program's cancellation, particularly the layoffs and the transfer of MOL crew members to NASA. While this is important information, the document could benefit from a more thorough exploration of the broader impact of the cancellation. This could include an analysis of the financial repercussions and the potential implications for future military space programs.

In conclusion, while the document provides valuable insights into the complexities and controversies surrounding the MOL program, it would benefit from a more critical analysis of the program's feasibility and effectiveness, a balanced representation of differing opinions surrounding the program, a more diverse range of personal accounts, and a deeper exploration of training programs, crew member roles, and responsibilities, as well as the wider consequences of the program's cancellation.

MAGA Perspective

The Manned Orbiting Laboratory (MOL) program is nothing but a wasteful endeavor by the United States Air Force to further its own agenda during the Cold War. Instead of focusing on more important issues such as national security and domestic needs, the government wasted precious resources on developing a space platform solely for military reconnaissance purposes. This program was a clear example of the government's disregard for fiscal responsibility.

Furthermore, the document fails to mention the potential negative consequences of the MOL program on international relations. By developing this military space platform, the United States only escalated tensions with other nations, especially the Soviet Union. It is irresponsible and dangerous to prioritize military advancements in space over diplomatic solutions and peaceful cooperation with other countries.

The document also downplays the role of technology and automation in space exploration. The insistence on sending humans into space for reconnaissance purposes is archaic and unnecessary. Advancements in remote sensing and robotics could have achieved the same objectives without putting human lives at risk. This outdated view of space exploration is a testament to the backward thinking prevalent in government institutions at the time.

It is disappointing that the document focuses heavily on the personal accounts of individuals involved in the MOL program and their reactions to its termination. While it may be unfortunate for those affected by the cancellation, it is essential to analyze and critique government programs based on their merits and broader implications. The emotional appeals presented in the document do not change the fact that the MOL program was an unnecessary and costly venture.

Overall, the document fails to acknowledge the criticisms and concerns surrounding the MOL program. It simply presents a one-sided narrative that glorifies the program while ignoring its flaws. As proponents of "Make America Great Again," we should focus on prioritizing practical and effective solutions that benefit all Americans, rather than indulging in vanity projects like the Manned Orbiting Laboratory program.

PAGE-BY-PAGE SUMMARIES

AI-2   *The Center for the Study of National Reconnaissance (CSNR) is an independent research body that aims to advance national reconnaissance and provide historical context for effective policy and programmatic decisions. Contact information and publication availability are provided.*

3   *This page provides a table of contents for a book titled "Spies in Space: Reflections on National Reconnaissance and the Manned Orbiting Laboratory." It includes chapters on the genesis and beginnings of MOL, the MOL pilots, and MOL up and running.*

4   *This page discusses the training, secrecy, and relationship with NASA of the Manned Orbiting Laboratory (MOL) program. It also covers the debate over the necessity of manned missions, budget challenges, and the termination of the MOL program.*

5   *This page discusses the Manned Orbiting Laboratory (MOL) program, a classified project by the National Reconnaissance Office (NRO) during the Cold War. The NRO recently declassified documents on the program, shedding light on the experiences and insights of those involved. The Dorian program, although not operational, had technological advancements that benefited future space and reconnaissance endeavors.*

7   *This book offers a first-hand account of the Manned Orbiting Laboratory program, which trained non-NASA individuals for reconnaissance purposes. It includes interviews with program participants and official documents, shedding light on a previously classified program.*

9   *This page discusses the potential advantages of manned space flight for intelligence collection and the development of the Manned Orbiting Laboratory's space imaging system. It also highlights various international crises where the United States faced limited intelligence collection capabilities.*

10   *The page discusses the Eisenhower administration's response to the Suez crisis and the Hungarian uprising, as well as the importance of intelligence in national security and foreign policy decisions. It also mentions the Cuban missile crisis and the US space program.*

11   *The Manned Orbiting Laboratory (MOL) program aimed to develop a manned reconnaissance platform in space for the US Air Force. Although it was ultimately cancelled, some MOL astronauts later joined NASA and flew on the Space Shuttle. The program faced challenges in terms of technology and cost.*

12   *The Manned Orbiting Laboratory program's legacy includes contributions to space and defense programs, technological development, and improved intelligence capabilities for the United States.*

13   *This page discusses the Manned Orbiting Laboratory (MOL) program and its goal of using manned spaceflight for national security. It also mentions the tensions between the Soviet Union and the United States during the Cold War and the urgency for the U.S. to catch up in the space race.*

14   *The page discusses the DynaSoar program, an experimental piloted vehicle designed to study re-entry from orbit and the sustainability of humans in space. It also mentions the Manned Orbiting Laboratory program, which aimed to explore military and reconnaissance capabilities in space.*

15   *The page discusses the development and termination of the DynaSoar program and the subsequent initiation of the Manned Orbiting Laboratory (MOL)*

	program by the Air Force. MOL was designed to be an orbiting laboratory for military astronauts to conduct experiments in space.
16	The page discusses concerns about the focus of the program office on manned reconnaissance systems and emphasizes the importance of specified objectives. Various studies were conducted to determine the best use and design for the program. The potential uses of man in space were identified as recognizing patterns and providing real-time image-motion.
17	The page discusses the Manned Orbiting Laboratory (MOL) program and its objectives, including high-resolution manned photoreconnaissance and conducting experiments in space. The Air Force distributed Request for Proposals to contractors and selected four for preliminary design studies.
18	The page discusses the early development of the Manned Orbiting Laboratory (MOL) program, including the establishment of guidelines for experiments and debates over the types of experiments to be included. It also mentions the proponents and critics of the MOL program.
19	The page discusses the importance and goals of the Manned Orbiting Laboratory (MOL) program, including its potential for improved military reconnaissance from space. The program faced skepticism regarding its ability to provide significant value compared to existing satellite photoreconnaissance programs.
20	The page discusses the debate over whether the Manned Orbiting Laboratory (MOL) program should be manned or unmanned. It highlights concerns about the political risks and security issues associated with a manned system, while also acknowledging the advantages of having a human presence in space.
21	The page discusses the challenges of maintaining secrecy for the Manned Orbiting Laboratory (MOL) program and proposes a hybrid approach of public announcement while maintaining covert reconnaissance objectives. It also addresses concerns about international reception and the need for specific guidelines for public affairs handling.
22	The page discusses the concerns and challenges surrounding the Manned Orbiting Laboratory (MOL) program, including potential international pushback and the need for tight control of information and publicity.
23	The page discusses the details and objectives of the proposed Manned Orbiting Laboratory (MOL) program, including its launch plans and mission duration. It also mentions the modified Titan IIIC booster and Gemini capsule that would be used in the program.
24	The page discusses the objectives and contractors involved in a program for assembling large structures and processing military equipment in space, emphasizing the importance of security and low-key public information.
25	The page discusses the approval and structure of the Manned Orbiting Laboratory (MOL) program, despite lack of universal support. It highlights the need for improved reconnaissance photography and the debate over how the program should be run. The page also mentions the public announcement of the MOL program by President Johnson.
26	The page discusses the public perception and concerns surrounding the Manned Orbiting Laboratory (MOL) program, as well as the establishment of a program office to oversee its development.

27	The page discusses the management structure and agreements made for the Manned Orbiting Laboratory (MOL), a classified reconnaissance mission disguised as an experimental orbiting laboratory run by the Air Force. The program involved both "black" and "white" aspects, with sensitive matters managed under the Director of SAFSP and mission planning handled by the Deputy Director of MOL. Several personnel changes also took place during this time.
28	The page discusses the management and development of the Manned Orbiting Laboratory (MOL) program, highlighting disagreements between key players and describing the design of the MOL spacecraft.
29	The page discusses the testing and integration process of the Manned Orbiting Laboratory (MOL) module, which was designed to be launched into space for reconnaissance purposes. It mentions the use of the Gemini B capsule and the Titan IIIM rocket for the mission.
31	The Manned Orbiting Laboratory (MOL) was a program that aimed to conduct high-resolution photography of the Soviet Union and other targets from space. Crew members would spend 30 days in the laboratory, taking photographs and participating in experiments. After the mission, the crew would return to Earth in a Gemini capsule, while the MOL hardware would be discarded. Recovery forces would be stationed around the world for emergency situations.
32	The Manned Orbiting Laboratory (MOL) plan included unmanned and manned flights to test and qualify the system. The flight schedule was adjusted, with some flights proposed to be unmanned. The schedule slipped by over a year.
33	The page discusses the debate over the role of crew members in the Manned Orbiting Laboratory (MOL) program and the contractors involved in the program's development.
34	The MOL Program Office underwent changes in management and structure as the program evolved. General Schriever retired, General Ferguson was named Director of MOL, and a new executive council was established. The program entered a new phase of development with definitive contracts signed. Concerns were raised about the current management structure, leading to proposed changes in responsibilities.
35	The page discusses the management changes and formation of committees for the Manned Orbiting Laboratory (MOL) program. It also mentions the appointment of Major General Joseph Bleymaier as Deputy Director and the selection of seventeen individuals to serve as MOL crew members.
41	The chapter discusses the selection process for the Manned Orbiting Laboratory (MOL) program, highlighting the highly selective and secretive nature of the process. It also mentions the physical considerations and tests that the candidates had to undergo.
42	The page discusses the selection process and secrecy surrounding the Manned Orbiting Laboratory (MOL) program, with interviews and briefings revealing the true nature of the program to the selected candidates.
43	The page discusses the selection and introduction of the first group of Manned Orbiting Laboratory (MOL) crew members in 1965. The Air Force held a press conference to introduce the eight crew members, but due to the classified nature of the program, it was intended to be the first and last interaction with the press.

44	The page provides information about the first group of astronauts selected for the Manned Orbiting Laboratory (MOL) program, including their backgrounds and experiences.
45	The page provides brief biographical information about three individuals, John Finley, Richard Lawyer, and Lachlan Macleay, who were selected for the Manned Orbiting Laboratory (MOL) program.
47	The selection process for the second group of Manned Orbiting Laboratory (MOL) pilots differed from the first group, as they had more knowledge about the program. The announcement of the second group was low-key and they had to wait for security clearance before fully joining the program. The first group welcomed the second group, although there were some divisions.
48	The page discusses the selection process for the second group of MOL pilots, with 25 candidates being screened and five ultimately selected. The names of the selected pilots are listed.
49	N/A
50	The page provides information about the background and selection process of the second and third groups of astronauts for the Manned Orbiting Laboratory (MOL) program. It mentions the names and backgrounds of several individuals who were selected for the program.
51	The page discusses the selection and background of James Alan Abrahamson, one of the astronauts in the third group of the Manned Orbiting Laboratory (MOL) program.
52	This page provides brief biographies of three individuals who were selected for the Manned Orbiting Laboratory (MOL) program: John B. Abrahamson, Robert Tralles Herres, and Robert Henry Lawrence, Jr. Lawrence, the first African American selected for spaceflight, tragically died in a training accident.
57	The Manned Orbiting Laboratory (MOL) program integrated astronauts into a space reconnaissance program, introducing new security concerns. The goals of the program were to obtain high-resolution photography and operational experience in space. Crew members were subject to strict regulations and limited public information.
58	The page discusses the roles and responsibilities of crew members in the Manned Orbiting Laboratory (MOL) program, including coordination with contractors and regular meetings to discuss tasks. Travel was also a significant part of the program.
59	Crew members of the Manned Orbiting Laboratory program worked on various aspects of the program, including developing a flight suit and working on simulations. Some crew members also focused on zero-gravity flights and testing methods for transferring between the Gemini capsule and the laboratory module.
60	Concerns about navigating the tunnel between the Gemini capsule and the laboratory module were addressed by training and the success of two astronauts. Bobko worked with engineers on various systems and provided valuable input during the design process. He was also supposed to work on measuring man's contribution to the MOL mission.
61	The page discusses the role of crew members in the Manned Orbiting Laboratory program, specifically their involvement in targeting and mission definition. The

	main goal was high resolution reconnaissance photography, with the crew playing a crucial role in image motion compensation and target selection.
63	The page discusses the operational concept and capabilities of the Manned Orbiting Laboratory (MOL), including target selection and prioritization, crew involvement in decision-making, and the development of software programs to facilitate the process.
64	The page discusses the role of astronauts in the Manned Orbiting Laboratory (MOL) program, specifically their involvement in targeting high-value photography targets and optimizing film usage. The crew's input and decision-making were crucial in achieving this goal.
65	The page discusses the role of manned missions in the Manned Orbiting Laboratory program, highlighting the belief that having a crew onboard would enhance the quality and quantity of intelligence gathered through photography. Man's presence was seen as vital for achieving superior photography and guaranteeing precision pointing.
66	The page discusses the training process for crew members of the MOL program, highlighting the different phases and simulators used to prepare them for various aspects of the mission. The training involved engineering work and assessing the feasibility of mission plans.
67	The page discusses the training methods used for the Manned Orbiting Laboratory program, including scuba diving and underwater simulations to prepare astronauts for the zero gravity environment of space.
68	MOL pilots underwent survival training, including water survival, in preparation for potential emergencies during missions. The training involved practicing in pressure suits and repairing rafts, with some pilots experiencing dangerous situations. The importance of proper training in the space program is emphasized.
69	Pilots in the Manned Orbiting Laboratory program undergo jungle survival training in Panama, learning to live off the wildlife and navigate through the jungle. They also experience a dangerous flash flood while floating down the Chagres River.
70	Crew members participated in NASA training and trained with Baltimore Colts players. They also received academic training in photographic intelligence. The MOL program was highly classified and concerns were raised about its impact on international relations.
71	The page discusses the secrecy and limited public information surrounding the Manned Orbiting Laboratory (MOL) program, including concerns about national security and potential misrepresentation. It also highlights the personal impact of program security on crew members and their families.
72	The page discusses the secrecy and relationship between the Manned Orbiting Laboratory (MOL) program and NASA during the early years of space exploration.
73	The page discusses the challenges and limited collaboration between the Manned Orbiting Laboratory (MOL) program and NASA due to security concerns. Despite this, there were some instances of cooperation, such as MOL flight surgeons supporting Apollo missions. The MOL program progressed with funding and support from various government agencies, and clear objectives were outlined for its development.

74	The MOL program had a successful year in 1968, with plans for future missions and potential contributions to intelligence and arms limitation agreements. However, it faced challenges that ultimately led to its downfall.
75	
81	The Manned Orbiting Laboratory (MOL) faced criticism and budget issues, leading to its cancellation. The debate over the necessity of manned space programs and their cost and risk was ongoing.
82	The page discusses the debate between using manned and unmanned systems for reconnaissance missions. Both options were explored, but ultimately a compromise was reached for concurrent development. However, there was later suggestion to pursue an unmanned-only system to save costs. The panel expressed disappointment in the lack of imagination in using man in a diagnostic role.
83	The page discusses the debate over the usefulness of manned systems in national reconnaissance, with concerns raised about their role as backups for automated systems and the increasing skepticism as unmanned technology improved.
84	The page discusses the debate over whether to use manned or unmanned systems for the MOL/Dorian program. It concludes that the manned system is more reliable and cost-effective, despite concerns over budget and technical risks.
85	The Soviet Union and international community had concerns that the Manned Orbiting Laboratory (MOL) program was a step towards militarizing space. The US State Department proposed allowing Soviet officials to inspect the MOL spacecraft for nuclear weapons, but this was strongly opposed by the Department of Defense. International concern affected the release of information about MOL.
86	The page discusses the debate over the necessity of Very High Resolution reconnaissance photography for national security. Critics argued that the high resolution photography available was adequate and that the MOL system was too expensive. The MOL Program Office produced a study to justify the value of Very High Resolution photography.
87	The page discusses the criticisms and concerns surrounding the Manned Orbiting Laboratory (MOL) program, including doubts about its value and potential duplicative efforts with NASA's Apollo program. Despite some supporters, MOL faced widespread skepticism.
88	The MOL program faced challenges and criticism for duplicating efforts with NASA's Apollo program. Budget constraints and competing priorities, such as the Vietnam War and Great Society programs, ultimately led to the demise of MOL.
89	The Manned Orbiting Laboratory (MOL) program faced significant budget cuts and funding deficits, resulting in schedule slips and potential reductions in manpower and technical tasks. Despite the rising costs, some believed that the program's benefits did not justify its expense.
90	The page discusses the budget and schedule issues faced by the Manned Orbiting Laboratory (MOL) program, which aimed to send astronauts into space. The program experienced funding cuts and schedule slips due to its high cost, making it difficult to justify its continuation.

91	The Manned Orbiting Laboratory (MOL) program faced numerous challenges in 1967 and 1968, including schedule slips and escalating costs. Eastman Kodak's delays were a major concern, and there were discussions about the possibility of switching to an unmanned development program. The frequent schedule slips caused frustration among crew members and led to some members leaving the program.
92	The Manned Orbiting Laboratory (MOL) program faced delays and skepticism, leading to its cancellation. Despite its potential contributions, the program took too long and struggled to justify its high costs and strict security measures.
93	The page discusses the challenges faced by the Manned Orbiting Laboratory (MOL) program, including lack of transparency and scrutiny from Congress. The program's value and cost were questioned, ultimately leading to its cancellation.
94	Supporters of the MOL program emphasized its progress and success despite challenges and criticisms.
95	The Manned Orbiting Laboratory (MOL) program was progressing well in 1968, with the launch facility nearing completion and progress being made on the Laboratory Module and software. However, there were criticisms and challenges that led to changes in the program's scope and design.
96	The page discusses the debate surrounding the cancellation of the Manned Orbiting Laboratory (MOL) program. The Bureau of the Budget argues that the program is too expensive and its contributions are becoming obsolete, while the MOL Program Office defends the program's value.
97	The page discusses the challenges and budget issues faced by the Manned Orbiting Laboratory (MOL) program, including suggestions to combine it with the Apollo Applications Program. The underfunding of MOL caused significant delays in its development.
98	The page discusses the underfunding and schedule delays of the Manned Orbiting Laboratory (MOL) program. It highlights the recommendation to cancel the manned portion of MOL and continue with an unmanned satellite system. The page also mentions the high costs invested in the program and the argument for the benefits of including manned capabilities.
99	The Manned Orbiting Laboratory (MOL) program, which aimed to enhance satellite reconnaissance, was terminated due to budget constraints and advancements in unmanned satellite systems. Despite its potential, MOL did not have immediate value compared to other Department of Defense programs.
100	The MOL program was terminated due to budget problems and schedule slips. The cancellation came as a shock to many involved, who were left unsure of their future plans.
101	The page discusses the cancellation of the Manned Orbiting Laboratory program, which came as a surprise to many involved. The decision was likely influenced by the success of unmanned systems and the focus on the civilian space program.
102	The page discusses the cancellation of the MOL program due to financial constraints, despite progress being made. It also mentions the reassignment of personnel and the possibility of some crew members joining NASA.
103	NASA took the seven youngest crew members from the Manned Orbiting Laboratory (MOL) to work on the space shuttle program, despite initially not

needing them. Some crew members chose to delay a year for further education. All seven eventually flew on the space shuttle.

104 The page discusses the selection process for NASA's astronaut program and the careers of those who were not selected. It also mentions the termination of the MOL program and the transfer of its hardware to NASA.

105 The page discusses the process of transferring assets from the Manned Orbiting Laboratory (MOL) program to NASA. It highlights the challenges and delays in the transfer, as well as the closure of MOL offices. The page also reflects on the lessons learned from the MOL program, emphasizing the importance of explaining progress and justifying the program's value.

106 The MOL program pushed boundaries and provided valuable experiences for young officers, despite being canceled before flying. The program emphasized understanding the entirety of a program and adapting to new challenges. Technology and lessons learned were transferred to other programs.

Notable Passages

5   "The Dorian program never became operational, but it was an investment by the National Reconnaissance Office in a technological program that had spin off's not only for America's future civilian space program, but in particular, also had high value for the practice of national reconnaissance. Many of NRO's future endeavors were dependent on and derived from the technologies that this program developed. But, perhaps more important was the Dorian program's investment in the people. Not only did its astronauts, who were more visible, gain experience, but many others in the program developed experience, gained insight, and then later in their career, used their unique experience to move the US forward in space and national reconnaissance."

9   "The National Reconnaissance Office recognized in the 1960's potential advantages of manned space flight for intelligence collection. The result was the development of the US Air Force's Manned Orbiting Laboratory's primary mission, the Dorian space imaging system. The purpose of the system was to overcome limitations of the photoreconnaissance satellites of the era, rapid tasking and evaluation of imagery to provide insight into crises faced by the United States. A manned space imagery system, in theory, would be more responsive to unanticipated events requiring immediate intelligence collection."

10   "However, the Cuban missile crisis confronted by the Kennedy administration brought the United States and the Soviet Union to the closest point during the Cold War of exchanging nuclear weapons. This crisis underscored the risks associated with limited means for collecting reliable, timely, and consistent intelligence in the nuclear age."

11   "Although the benefits of the program, if successful, would significantly improve US intelligence collection capabilities, the challenges for successfully carrying out the program were daunting. The manned space program required levels of assurance much greater than unmanned space programs. This alone increased both the time and expense in developing the MOL program. Additionally, the NRO program for MOL, known as Dorian, required technological breakthroughs that had not yet been achieved, including a target spotting mechanism in advance of the actual imaging, development of the images on orbit, and target management systems. The MOL astronauts worked diligently on these and other challenges to make the system work."

12   "The most significant contribution is that the MOL helped better position the United States to be less likely surprised by international crises and threats, and better able to respond to the international challenges faced by the nation through the availability of better and timelier intelligence. The Manned Orbiting Laboratory program and those who served in the program contributed to a base of knowledge that continues to be built upon for today's critical and unique national reconnaissance systems."

13   "The fantasy of flying in space became the American imperative."

14	"In late 1961, under the direction of the new Secretary of Defense Robert McNamara, officials reoriented DynaSoar. The spaceplane, re-designated the X-20, would now be launched into full orbit. The main objective of the program remained studying the maneuverability of re-entry from orbit, in addition to studying the sustainability of man in space."
15	"In initiating the MOL program, it was decided to terminate the DYNASOAR (X-20) program because the current requirement is for a program aimed directly at the basic question of man's utility in space, rather than a program limited to finding means to control the return of man from space. The DYNASOAR Program was designed to do the latter."
16	"It is absolutely crucial to the survival of this program that it be directed at the start to specified and fully approved objectives, and that it be held to these objectives until they are accomplished or changed. Development of a manned reconnaissance system is not an approved objective."
17	n/a
18	"...putting man in the position of a pointer not a thinker..."
19	"The importance of the MOL program dictates that the Air Force investigate alternatives for shortening the development cycle."
20	"With regard to the MOL proposal itself, the Air Force has done an exceedingly thorough analysis of both the manned and unmanned system alternatives for a high resolution optical reconnaissance system. It has, in my opinion, documented a persuasive argument that, for equal total weights and total volumes, the manned system does have an advantage over the unmanned system and can be expected to provide a higher average resolution at an earlier time than the unmanned system."
21	"In view of the fact that a good deal of information about the MOL has already been made public through Congressional hearings and public statements, it would clearly not be reasonable to expect that the general characteristics, purpose, and success or failure of its launches will not be made public. I am, therefore, inclined to believe that most aspects of the MOL program will have to be conducted with reasonable openness. At the same time, there may be aspects which it would be preferable to put under specific restraints. In short, I believe the MOL program requires specific guidelines of its own for public affairs handling and in turn may pose particular foreign policy issues."
22	"disclosure of the MOL reconnaissance capability is an irreversible step which would have profound adverse effects on enemies, allies, and neutrals. Furthermore, no gain would appear to flow from disclosure."
23	"MOL's objectives were primarily 'to secure photographs of [superior] resolutions of significant targets,' to develop 'high-resolution optical technology and systems for either manned or unmanned use,' to provide 'a facility for the development, test and use of other potential military applications.'"
24	"Working toward those objectives, McNamara reinforced the necessity of security to prevent international concerns, keeping public information modest and low key."
25	"I believe that there is a vital national need for reconnaissance photography at a resolution of [superior] or better," arguing that it would be used for improved technical intelligence, in times of crisis, and in better policing arms control agreements. Likewise, the improved resolution would undoubtedly provide the U.S. with a better assessment of Soviet and Chinese capabilities and technology.

	McNamara concluded, "My judgment is that we should now proceed to acquire the benefits of an experimental manned system."
26	"This program will bring us new knowledge about what man is able to do in space. It will enable us to relate that ability to the defense of America. It will develop technology and equipment which will help advance manned and unmanned space flights. And it will make it possible to perform their new and rewarding experiments with that technology and equipment."
27	"MOL represented a unique management problem, broad in both scope and complexity with a program structure quite different from that of previous satellite reconnaissance programs."
28	"Although agreements were reached early, these divisions were messy, and disagreements plagued the management office. Shortly after the initial agreement was signed between General Schriever and Brig. Gen. Martin, Colonel Worthman summarized the situation in a memorandum by stating the generals' positions as, 'General Evans: 'If I'm running the MOL Program, I expect to run all parts of it and to direct all participants.' General Martin: 'The Dorian Program is run by the Director, NRO. My guidance and direction comes solely from him." Colonel Worthman went on to note, 'These differences are fundamental and may be irresolvable.'"
29	"We had taken a regular Gemini that NASA had designed and was flying, and [we] cut a hatch in the ablative heat shield that protects you on the re-entry. There was some concern as to whether that would cause the shield not to be able to do its job, so there was a test flight that was flown to go check that out."
30	n/a
31	"The only approved and funded mission of the MOL program is that of very high resolution optical photographic reconnaissance in support of National Reconnaissance Program objectives."
32	n/a
33	"The idea was humans could help pick targets in real time, they could identify cloud cover and save film. The system was resource-limited because it was a film system, not electronic like we have now. But the whole idea was to have a far more capable intelligence capability because you had people there that could think and act and take action in real time during the flight."
34	"It has become increasingly apparent that present assignments of program responsibilities to SAFSP and the MOL Systems Office are not conducive to the best possible Government management of this complex and costly system... It is now proposed to assign essentially all base-line program responsibility to the MOL Systems Office."
35	"Let's build this damn thing and make it work."
41	"I didn't volunteer to get on the list. In other words, there was, to my knowledge, no open application process to get on MOL."
42	"Through all the tests and physicals and interviews, no one knew exactly what they were getting into...We had been selected and then at least a month into the program before we were ever briefed on the reconnaissance mission...The layers of secrecy started to fall away after they were announced and their clearances came through...It was one of the most amazing days of my entire career because we got briefed on all these code words...And of course at that time, the NRO was covert, none of these organizations existed. None of the programs existed in the

	public eye. And yet they were doing great things. It gave me great confidence in the United States that they could pull off such an enormous technological effort and still be invisible."
44	"I decided then that I wanted to be an astronaut."
47	"It didn't exist. It was all highly classified and compartmentalized programs. You had a 'need to know.' It was the kind of thing where you had to get a personal introduction to anybody to even talk about the program."
50	"He developed Maxwell's equations from the start. That's all I needed, was to sit there and watch. He was smart as a whip."
53	"It was a fun time, it really was. I really loved it."
57	"The main goals for the MOL program were going to be to get high resolution photography and to get some data, operational experience in the space arena."
59	"The crew was each given particular areas to go work on and follow, put in crew input, controls in this place. I worked very hard with Douglas on the controls for the laboratory. We were building a simulator at General Electric to be able to do some of the training for the classified work. I worked on that as well."
60	"It was a challenge to be able to climb from the Gemini back through an 18-inch hole into the laboratory. Then later on, you had to come back the other way, and both times you were in a pressure suit doing that. We trained for it, and of course all of us didn't do it. But two guys, going through the hole, did do it on the zero-G airplane the best it could be done. Of course all the rest of us knew that if those guys could do it, we could do it."
61	"The main goal of the program was to attain high resolution reconnaissance photography, so how did man fit into that? Macleay explained that their concept 'became kind of the basis for the manned interface and how we were going to help select targets. We actually had two things to do: one was image motion compensation to get the best resolution you could get. The other was target selection.' Both crew members were essential. Truly explained, 'You had a commander and a pilot... Once we got on orbit, it was strictly a team operation. Both guys had to know how to do everything.'"
63	"We developed a concept and then a capability [for the] two crew. If they were going over a target area, we had two telescopes that were high-powered telescopes. I don't remember what resolution they were, but [they] could jump from potential target to potential target."
64	"To me that was one of the things that was most important about [MOL], was to use the crew to go ahead and filter out a lot of these places so you didn't take pictures of them, you didn't waste film."
65	"To have a crew onboard, you could have somebody looking at what's happening and decide whether or not they want to take a photo or other data of whatever it is that you're watching... Selection of data, I think, is one of the big things, that you can have somebody knowledgeable look at this."
66	"I would say that we never got into what I would call a 'training phase.' We were busy doing engineering kind of work... It wasn't training so much as it was assessing whether we could do some of the things we were being asked to do."
68	"That's one of the interesting things about the space program, that you do so many different kinds of training, either airplanes or survival or parachuting or whatever. And any one of them, you do it wrong, it can get you."

69	"For the crew, survival school was about learning vital skills and also enjoying training with friends. Macleay remembered, 'We had built what we called the officer's club... It had a fire pit and little shed over a bench we could sit on. We built all that there. We had our fire going one night and a bat flew through, and Hank Hartsfield jumped right in my lap; it scared the hell out of him. In the meantime, there were all these guides trying to catch you, all the natives. You had a hat, and if they got your hat, they could turn the hat in for $5 or something. So they were looking for you.'"
70	"The MOL system was unique in its design to utilize man to help select active and significant reconnaissance targets, and the NPIC training was essential in training man to be effective in this role."
71	"It was hard to talk about anything, just about everything was covered under the secrecy of 'It's the MOL program,' and that's about when everybody shut up."
72	"Secrecy was so ingrained in those involved in the program that 35 years after MOL was canceled, when asked about the reconnaissance mission, Bobko explained, 'I'm still a little edgy about talking about it because nobody's ever talked about it.'"
73	"In addition to competition over resources and priority, MOL security concerns proved a nearly insurmountable barrier to developing a cooperative relationship with NASA. Truly summarized, 'NASA worked as hard to get publicity as the NRO did to avoid publicity.' Reflecting on the relationship, Abrahamson commented, 'In MOL, we should have been much closer to NASA, but we felt like we couldn't because of the classification of the program. We saw them, they knew we existed, and we'd try to get to know each other and listen. But we couldn't talk about it very much. So in that sense, it was hard.'"
74	"MOL has some potential to obtain coverage of targets or areas during periods of international tension and crisis. During the Cuban missile crisis, the value of VHR photography to provide easily understood and incontrovertible evidence for national decision making was clearly demonstrated. MOL will be on orbit about 25 per cent of the time during the year and can pass daily over a point of interest with little penalty."
81	"Facing major budget issues and inadequate support, MOL's critics eventually succeeded, and the program was canceled before it ever had a chance to prove its worth."
82	"The DIAMOND II study, comparing the anticipated successful reconnaissance products achieved through the manned and unmanned systems, resulted in a 91-page report. The study found that by using man as a weather scout, 'A manned DORIAN system will successfully photograph approximately 18-20 percent more targets than an unmanned system when employed on identical intelligence-collection missions against average Sino-Soviet Bloc climatology.'"
83	"The presence of the crew in the initial flights of the MOL system will, by virtue of their abilities to perform switching, maintenance, manual backup, and in particular, diagnostic functions in situations of failure or off-nominal performance, significantly contribute to an early maturing of the unmanned system. At the same time, the missions will simultaneously be gathering high-resolution photography of significant intelligence value."
84	"The absence of man increases the development risk..."
85	"While many nations have recognized the significant potential offered by this project in the further peaceful exploration of space, we regret that the Soviet

86   Union has taken a view to the contrary, alleging that it is just another manifestation of a U.S. intention to use outer space for other than peaceful purposes."

86   "The United States has a vital need for intelligence information pertaining to activities/developments within the Sino-Soviet [sic] and other denied areas. For various intelligence purposes, the types, quality, and quantity of information to be collected vary considerably, and therefore, a multiplicity of programs are contributing toward the fulfillment of the overall objective. Of significant importance to the total intelligence picture is the need for very high-resolution photographic coverage primarily for technical intelligence purposes, and it is to this purpose that the MOL/DORIAN Program is oriented."

87   "In the face of widespread criticism, advocates of the program remained. Director of Defense Research and Engineering John S. Foster, Jr. stated, 'My conclusion, as presented in the most recent MOL DCP, that the value to DoD of MOL very high resolution photography combined with its mission flexibility justifies the remaining development and estimated operating costs; and my recommendation for proceeding with the baseline (manned and unmanned) program were supported by the Secretary of the Air Force, the President's Scientific Advisor, the Director of the DIA, the Director of the National Reconnaissance Program, and the Assistant Secretary (Comptroller) and approved by the Deputy Secretary of Defense.' But even with this impressive list of supporters, MOL continued to be

88   "In summary, it can be seen that the Apollo Applications Program and MOL Program are different and complementary; they are not competitive in mission and are not redundant in terms of hardware development."

89   "I can't seem to refrain from 'selling' MOL."

90   "When asked about the schedule slips, Macleay explained, 'It was money. It was just flat money.' Karol Bobko recalled, 'There were a number of times when we had slips because of inadequate funding, and so everybody was worried about that. I can remember one time that they had a study, and it showed that it didn't do any good to slip for less than three months because it took you three months to get squared away after you slipped. And then they slipped for three months.' The budget crisis and ensuing schedule slips were seemingly endless."

91   "In my opinion, this will result in the program position being even more precarious than it is already."

92   "The manned MOL program, despite unquestionable talent and significant potential contributions, was taking too long."

93   "It is questionable as to whether we can gain and/or maintain the necessary interest in and support for the MOL program among concerned Congressional, military and professional groups and still adhere to currently exercised security policy and briefing procedures."

94   "In addition to justifying MOL's existence, supporters also emphasized that MOL was on track and progressing. Maj. Gen. Bleymaier conducted a briefing with the new DNRO John McLucas in April 1969 emphasizing 'that the program was on schedule, that there were no technical problems, progress was measurable, management tools and relationships between the government and contractors are adequate and satisfactory.' Despite a myriad of challenges and criticisms, supporters continued to advocate for the program and MOL continued."

95   "In one meeting, 227 items were submitted, and 213 items were approved."

96   "Given the state of the program, Foster divided the problem into three questions. First, should MOL be canceled? Second, if the program were to continue, should the unmanned system be canceled? Lastly, if the program were to continue, what should the financial support to the program look like for FY 1970? Exploring these issues, Foster argued that MOL's mission flexibility and VHR contributions – including monitoring arms limitation agreements and obtaining coverage of targets during times of crisis – justified MOL and its expenses. With that said, Foster recommended that MOL be funded its full amount of $575 million for FY 1970 and the unmanned option remain part of MOL."

97   "Seamans argued the four-flight plan 'would protect, with minimum commitment, until December 1970 a continuing very high resolution operational reconnaissance capability in the 1970s, provide time in which to carefully assess other options, and sustain a minimum cost development program leading to manned or unmanned operational systems.'"

98   "I recommend a reorientation of this program as follows: We should continue to develop the MOL camera system as part of an unmanned, covert satellite system in the National Reconnaissance Program. We should cancel all elements of the overt Manned Orbiting Laboratory Program and announce that we are doing this partly to conserve funds, partly because the program has slipped 2 ½ years since first start, and partly because we can now pursue many of the original objectives with less expensive, unmanned systems."

99   "The MOL Program is currently progressing well. It is totally defined, and all engineering is understood… The Program is meeting all schedule dates, and detailed test results of critical components indicate that system performance specifications required to meet the [superior] resolution goal will be met or exceeded."

100 "When they canceled the program, they called everybody into the auditorium and just said, 'It's canceled.' I don't know what happened. I think it surprised everybody. I thought that when it was canceled, we had a fairly good mission, and we were really starting to work towards our goal. And then it was canceled out of the blue."

101 "We were in a SCIF up at GE in King of Prussia, and I was sitting at a table arguing with a guy who I think worked for McDonnell Douglas. We were arguing, literally, over a bit in a software program. We were arguing about the smallest piece of the space program, a single line of code in Gemini. I can't even remember what it was. Anyway, I was sitting there arguing this, it was about 10 in the morning, and Mac walked in the conference room and tapped me on the shoulder. I looked up at him and I said, 'Wait a minute, back up, I'm about to win this argument.' He jabbed my shoulder and I looked around to him and he said,

102 "We just ran out of time, ran out of money, we weren't getting there. Because we weren't getting any closer to the launch, they were just kind of pouring money down a rat hole, as far as they were concerned."

104 "The MOL program had attracted uniquely talented and ambitious crew members. Even after the program was canceled, those crew members continued to serve their country and pursue impressive careers."

105 "I don't care how far along the program is, it can go away in a heartbeat."

106   "The MOL program was designed to push boundaries – to gain needed intelligence and explore what man could do from space. While development faced major hurdles and the program was canceled before it ever had a chance to fly, MOL was a proving ground for young officers, and all walked away from the program better prepared for the future. Technology was transferred to other programs, and crew members, shaped by their experiences on MOL, applied their knowledge and experience to new programs. Although the program was canceled, the technology developed and lessons learned were invaluable. Dick Truly reflected fondly, 'It was an amazing experience for a young officer.'"

SPIES IN SPACE:
REFLECTIONS ON NATIONAL RECONNAISSANCE AND THE MANNED ORBITING LABORATORY

by Courtney V. K. Homer

CENTER FOR THE STUDY OF
NATIONAL RECONNAISSANCE

MAY 2019

CENTER FOR THE STUDY OF NATIONAL RECONNAISSANCE

The Center for the Study of National Reconnaissance (CSNR) is an independent National Reconnaissance Office (NRO) research body reporting to the Director/Business Plans and Operations Directorate, NRO. The CSNR's primary objective is to advance national reconnaissance and make available to NRO leadership the analytic framework and historical context to make effective policy and programmatic decisions. The CSNR accomplishes its mission by promoting the study, dialogue, and understanding of the discipline, practice, and history of national reconnaissance. The CSNR studies the past, analyzes the present, and searches for lessons for the future.

Contact Information: Phone, 703-227-9368; or e-mail, csnr@nro.mil

To Obtain Copies: Government personnel may obtain additional printed copies directly from CSNR. Other requesters may purchase printed copies by contacting the Government Publishing Office. Selected CSNR publications are available on the Internet at the NRO web site.

Published by

NATIONAL RECONNAISSANCE OFFICE
Center for the Study of National Reconnaissance
14675 Lee Road
Chantilly, Virginia 20151 1715

For sale by the Superintendent of Documents, U.S. Government Publishing Office
Internet: bookstore.gpo.gov Phone: toll free (866) 512-1800 DC area (202) 512-1800
Fax: (202) 512-2104 Mail: Stop IDCC Washington, D.C. 20402-0001
ISBN: 978-1-937219-24-6

TABLE OF CONTENTS

FOREWORD v
PREFACE vii
INTRODUCTION ix

CHAPTER 1
THE GENESIS & BEGINNINGS OF MOL 1
- DynaSoar 1
- The MOL Concept and End of DynaSoar 2
- Early Studies 3
- MOL Experiments 5
- MOL's Proponents and Critics 7
- MOL and the Public 8
- MOL on the International Stage 9
- MOL Takes Shape 11
- The Program Office 13
- MOL Goes Public 13
- Establishing a Program Office 14
- The Mechanics of MOL 16
- MOL Contractors 21
- An Updated Management Approach 22
- Endnotes 24

CHAPTER 2
THE MOL PILOTS 29
- Selecting the First Group 29
- The First Group of MOL Pilots 31
- Selecting the Second Group 35
- The Second Group of MOL Pilots 36
- Selecting the Third Group 38
- The Third Group of MOL Pilots 39
- Endnotes 42

CHAPTER 3
MOL UP AND RUNNING 45
- Integrating Man 45
- Individual Roles 46
- A New Concept For Man 49
- The Role of the Astronaut 52

Training the Crew 54
Water Training 55
Survival Training 56
Cross-Organizational Training 58
MOL's Secrecy 58
MOL's Relationship with NASA 60
The MOL Build-Up 61
Endnotes 63

CHAPTER 4
THE END OF MOL 69
The Debate over the Necessity of Man 69
The Soviet Concern 73
The Importance of Very High Resolution Reconnaissance 74
The NASA/DoD Overlap 75
Budget Challenges 76
MOL's Slipping Schedule 78
Justifying MOL 80
MOL Continues 83
Talk of Cancellation 84
Terminating MOL 87
MOL's Termination and its People 90
MOL's Termination and its Hardware 92
Looking Back and Lessons Learned 93
Endnotes 95

INDEX 103

FOREWORD

In December 1963, while a student at New York University in its Air Force ROTC program, I was intrigued by a press release by the Air Force. The release had announced that the Air Force was developing something called the Manned Orbiting Laboratory (MOL). It was a program being developed to "... increase the Defense Department effort to determine military usefulness of men in space." This was a new domain for ROTC students to explore—Astronauts with a military mission! While I, my fellow students, and the public saw this merely as another major move forward by the US in its very public "space race" with the Soviet Union, little did we know that there was a hidden, highly classified aspect to the MOL effort. It was "Dorian," a deeply classified program managed by the then darkly hidden agency of the Intelligence Community, the National Reconnaissance Office (NRO).

Fifty-two years later, on 22 October 2015 I had the honor of meeting five of these NRO astronauts (James Abrahamson, Karol Bobko, Albert Crews, Bob Crippen, and Richard Truly), along with the program's technical director, Michael Yarymovych. These five pioneering individuals were members of a panel that I was moderating at the National Museum of the United States Air Force (NMUSAF) in Dayton, OH.

The NRO's Center for the Study of National Reconnaissance (CSNR) was holding the panel on the occasion of the NRO declassifying almost its entire collection of records on the Dorian program. There were over 850 documents with some 22,000 pages and 280 photographs. It had taken over a year for the NRO's declassification center to do its line-by-line review of the collection. As a part of the declassification effort, the CSNR had published a compilation of declassified Dorian documents in a compendium, which the Senior NRO Historian and Deputy Director of CSNR, Dr. James D. Outzen, had edited.*

The compendium included Carl Berger's earlier MOL history, which is a record of the administrative efforts to develop and sustain the MOL Program. This current book, *Spies in Space—Reflections on National Reconnaissance and the Manned Orbiting Laboratory*, goes well beyond that. The CSNR Oral Historian, Courtney Homer, conducted many hours of research, with a focus on oral history interviews. She based this new history on those interviews, as well as the findings from her additional documentary research.

This book offers the reader a window into the experiences and insight of those who were training to be America's spies in space during the Cold War. It is the recollections of those who lived the Dorian and MOL experience.

The Dorian program never became operational, but it was an investment by the National Reconnaissance Office in a technological program that had spin off's not only for America's future civilian space program, but in particular, also had high value for the practice of national reconnaissance. Many of NRO's future endeavors were dependent on and derived from the technologies that this program developed. But, perhaps more important was the Dorian program's investment in the people. Not only did its astronauts, who were more visible, gain experience, but many others in the program developed experience, gained insight, and then later in their career, used their unique experience to move the US forward in space and national reconnaissance.

Robert A. McDonald, Ph.D.
Director, CSNR/Emeritus
Chantilly, VA

---

* See Outzen, J. D., Ed. (2015), *The Dorian Files Revealed: A Compendium of the NRO's Manned Orbiting Laboratory Documents*, Chantilly, VA: CSNR (printed by US Government Printing Office). On the day after the panel, the NRO's Information Review and Release Group (IRRG) posted its declassified collection on the NRO public web page.

PREFACE

Between 1965 and 1969, quietly and without fanfare, 17 non-NASA individuals were astronaut-trained in order to meet the reconnaissance needs of the United States. They came from across the military services. Participants in the Manned Orbiting Laboratory program trained tirelessly and worked relentlessly because they believed they could contribute something unique to U.S. reconnaissance efforts and because they all shared a dream of flying in space.

The purpose of this book is to offer a first-hand account of the MOL program for the first time. Shrouded in secrecy, the MOL program was declassified by the National Reconnaissance Office in 2015. This is the first opportunity many participants had to share their experiences with anyone outside their small cadres.

The bulk of the book is written in their words, taken directly from transcripts of oral history interviews conducted over the last five years with program participants, as well as official documents and transcripts written by the officers who participated in and managed the programs. Thank you to James Abrahamson, Karol Bobko, Albert Crews, Robert Crippen, Lachlan Macleay, and Richard Truly for giving of your time, and in some cases, opening your homes to me. Every interview offered a new perspective and new insight, and I am indebted to each of them. An additional thank you goes to Michael Yarymovych, MOL's technical director, who shared his insights from a program management point of view. This project would not be possible without the hours they spent with me sharing their stories and experiences, their insights and their disappointments.

In addition, this book would not be possible without the support and vision of the CSNR staff and management. Thank you to James Outzen, the Director of CSNR, who entrusted me with this project; he advised and consulted, and he allowed it to grow into the two-volume publication we have today. Thank you to CSNR's talented graphic artist, Chuck Glover, who turned a manuscript into a book and never let an edit annoy him. And thank you to Mike Suk, who edited ruthlessly and necessarily. This is a far better publication because of his input.

Although the program was cancelled far sooner than participants and program leadership hoped, both programs served as a unique training ground for the individuals who would go on to see remarkable success. This is their story.

Courtney V. K. Homer
CSNR Oral Historian

INTRODUCTION

The National Reconnaissance Office recognized in the 1960's potential advantages of manned space flight for intelligence collection. The result was the development of the US Air Force's Manned Orbiting Laboratory's primary mission, the Dorian space imaging system. The purpose of the system was to overcome limitations of the photoreconnaissance satellites of the era, rapid tasking and evaluation of imagery to provide insight into crises faced by the United States. A manned space imagery system, in theory, would be more responsive to unanticipated events requiring immediate intelligence collection.

In the wake of World War II, the United States still had few intelligence collection means responsive to unexpected events of concern for the security and interests of the nation. This deficiency was clear as Israel declared its independence on 14 May 1948 and troops from neighboring Arab states moved against Israeli forces the next day, initiating the 1948 Arab-Israeli War. The United States supported the establishment of Israel, recognizing the new state within minutes of its declaration of statehood. The US also anticipated that neighboring Arab nations would not idly standby with the declaration and subsequent US recognition. Nonetheless, as the nations battled each other, the US leadership had few objective means of gaining intelligence in this war lasting until the summer of 1949.

The summer of 1948 brought another crisis for the United States to respond to as the Soviet Union instituted a blockade of sections of Berlin occupied by the US, Great Britain, and France. Disagreement and tensions increased between the Soviet Union and western powers over the control and governance of defeated Germany in the months following World War II. By 1948, the western powers were supportive of German self-government and determination, contrary to the desires of the Soviet Union. With the western advocacy for new currency that would help lift the German economy and its self-sufficiency, the Soviet Union instituted the blockade of Berlin hoping to force western powers' capitulation on German rebuilding. Again, the United States faced an international crisis with limited intelligence collection to assist in the most effective management of the crisis.

Early on Sunday morning of 25 June 1950, the United States was again surprised by the seemingly sudden attack of communist North Korean forces against weaker South Korean forces. In the early days of the conflict, it appeared that North Korea would quickly vanquish the South Korean forces and extinguish democracy on the peninsula. Under the auspices of the United Nations, the Truman administration committed US forces to repel the North Koreans, leaving the United States engaged in a war that would only conclude some three years later after the election of a new US president, Dwight Eisenhower.

As with any US president, Eisenhower would face significant international crises; however, the fall of 1956 proved to be an exceptionally difficult period. On 29 October 1956, Israeli troops moved into the Sinai, setting the stage for a combined British, French, and Israeli effort to destabilize Egyptian president Nasser's government through takeover of the Suez canal. Earlier in the summer, Nassar had nationalized the canal, removing British controls over the vital transportation link for oil exports to Great Britain and France. Great Britain and France coordinated military plans with Israel to carry out multi-pronged military action against Egypt. Those combined nations believed that the Eisenhower administration would not counter the military attacks of Great Britain, France, and Israel against Nassar's Egypt. Although caught off guard by the attacks, Eisenhower did strongly condemn them. He ordered economic sanctions against Israel and sought votes in the United Nations condemning the military activity. By the spring of 1957, all sides agreed to a ceasefire with the United Nations providing member nation troops to keep peace along the Suez.

While responding to the Suez crisis, the Eisenhower administration also was responding to an uprising of Hungarians against the Soviet backed communist government in Hungary. The uprising began on 24 October 1956 when a group of mostly university students called for Hungary to back out of the Warsaw Pact and become a neutral or non-aligned nation like neighboring Austria. The students were emboldened by recent events in Poland that suggested the Soviet Union would not block a change in Hungarian international political alliances. The protests quickly grew, resulting in attacks on Soviet troops and Hungarian secret police. Imar Nagy emerged as the new Hungarian leader, who at first had Soviet backing. But as Nagy pursued a policy of leaving the Warsaw Pact, the Soviet Union withdrew its support and, by 4 November, reinforced Soviet troops already in Hungary, leading to the collapse of the Nagy government and the uprising. During the crises, the Eisenhower administration depended almost exclusively on newspaper accounts to manage the crisis.

Eisenhower recognized the importance of intelligence for making sound national security and foreign policy decisions. His views, like many who led during the early years of the Cold War, were shaped not only by world events in the late 1940s and 1950s, but also by the absence of actionable intelligence on Japanese activities in preparation for their surprise attack on Pearl Harbor. Eisenhower wanted no such attacks during his stewardship of the nation as president. Accordingly, he approved a number of intelligence collection systems including the high altitude reconnaissance U-2 aircraft and the nation's first satellite reconnaissance programs, Samos and Corona. Other innovative programs were also pursued during this time period, including the US Air Force's X-20 Dyna-Soar space plane, a reusable manned space vehicle. Through these and other programs, the United States sought the advantages of observing the earth for defense of US interests.

The importance of gaining consistent and reliable intelligence would be further punctuated by the Cuban missile crisis in October 1962. Of all the threats to the United States, nuclear weapons posed the greatest danger. Although the Truman administration knew that the Soviets were pursuing a nuclear bomb, they were surprised with the first successful Soviet nuclear test that occurred in August 1949—a test that occurred years earlier than US intelligence estimates anticipated. Eisenhower would witness during his first year in office the first test of a Soviet hydrogen bomb, again well in advance of intelligence estimates at the time. However, the Cuban missile crisis confronted by the Kennedy administration brought the United States and the Soviet Union to the closest point during the Cold War of exchanging nuclear weapons. This crisis underscored the risks associated with limited means for collecting reliable, timely, and consistent intelligence in the nuclear age.

In parallel to the emerging threat of nuclear weapons, the United States and the Soviet Union were investing heavily in their space programs. President Kennedy's 1962 call to put a man on the moon by the end of the decade accelerated the US's manned space program. This acceleration prompted consideration of how a manned space presence may be used to advance US interests. Although NASA carried out the US' programs for space exploration and manned space flight with the goal of reaching the moon, this did not preclude the US Air Force from considering manned space flight as a means for advancing US national security and defense interests. In this environment, the US Department of Defense announced in 1963 the establishment of the US Air Forces' Manned Orbiting Laboratory, and thereby the intent to develop a manned space program for military defense purposes.

By 1965, the US Air Force had selected its first military officers to participate in the MOL program. Among those selected was Al Crews, who transferred from the recently cancelled Dyna-Soar program. Eventually 16 other individuals would join Crews as MOL astronauts. They would not only train to prepare for manned space flight, but also take on specific responsibilities for developing technologies and components necessary for the program. They would form a close association during this period of program training and development.

Although the US Air Force announced the MOL project, they did not disclose the primary purpose of the program—to serve as a manned reconnaissance platform in space. Instead, the Air Force disclosed that the platform would be used for space experiments. During the early planning stages of the MOL program, the US Air Force sought a compelling reason for developing the program given NASA's mandate for manned space flight. The newly formed National Reconnaissance Office provided the most compelling reason for a military manned space program, putting a high resolution telescope into space to observe the activities of the Soviet Union and other US adversaries.

At the time MOL was under development, the United States had already demonstrated that imagery and signals intelligence from space satellites provided compelling insight to US leaders, including the president. The limitations, especially of photoreconnaissance satellites, included timeliness of the intelligence and capture of the intelligence in optimal weather conditions. Photoreconnaissance satellites captured images on film that took days to weeks to be deorbited, processed, analyzed, and made available to senior US leadership. Often the imagery was of limited value because of persistent cloud cover over areas of interest to the US. A manned imagery collection system in space seemed an elegant solution for overcoming these limitations. In theory, national reconnaissance astronauts could spot targets of interest, especially in a crisis, and image on orbits where those areas of interest were free of cloud cover. The astronauts could then develop and provide a preliminary readout of conditions on the ground in a crisis situation. If successful, the MOL program would provide intelligence information that would otherwise not be available for critical US decision-making.

Although the benefits of the program, if successful, would significantly improve US intelligence collection capabilities, the challenges for successfully carrying out the program were daunting. The manned space program required levels of assurance much greater than unmanned space programs. This alone increased both the time and expense in developing the MOL program. Additionally, the NRO program for MOL, known as Dorian, required technological breakthroughs that had not yet been achieved, including a target spotting mechanism in advance of the actual imaging, development of the images on orbit, and target management systems. The MOL astronauts worked diligently on these and other challenges to make the system work.

In the end, none of the MOL astronauts flew on the program. It was cancelled in favor of better unmanned photoreconnaissance satellites and the promise of near real-time electro-optical imagery. Nonetheless, several of the MOL astronauts did join NASA and flew on the Space Transportation System or the Space Shuttle as it was known. Those individuals included future NASA administer Richard Truly, future Kennedy Space Center Director and pilot of the first Shuttle mission, Bob Crippen, and serving as Shuttle pilots and/or commanders, Karol Bobko and Henry Hartsfield. All of those individuals joined Al Crews along with Lachlan Macleay in sharing their memories for this project. James Abrahamson who would lead the DoD's Strategic Defense initiative also provided recollections for this project.

Although the MOL program was cancelled, its legacy continued not only through the contributions to US space and defense programs by the astronauts who trained for the program, but also the technological development from the program. The technology investments in MOL were transferred to NASA for its own manned laboratory program that launched in the 1970s. The NRO also directly benefited in investments in both launch and reconnaissance collection systems that would mature for use in other NRO programs.

The most significant contribution is that the MOL helped better position the United States to be less likely surprised by international crises and threats, and better able to respond to the international challenges faced by the nation through the availability of better and timelier intelligence. The Manned Orbiting Laboratory program and those who served in the program contributed to a base of knowledge that continues to be built upon for today's critical and unique national reconnaissance systems.

James D. Outzen, Ph.D.
Director, Center for the Study of National Reconnaissance

Chapter 1

THE GENESIS & BEGINNINGS OF MOL

Flying in space – the exhilaration of liftoff, floating in zero-gravity, observing the earth – is a dream of many and a reality of few. This is the story of those who aspired to spaceflight, who believed that during a time of fear and uncertainty, their mission would strengthen our national defense and make the United States a safer place in which to live. The Manned Orbiting Laboratory (MOL) Program was centered on the idea that man could be useful in space and that reconnaissance from space was essential for the country's national security. Ultimately neither program was given what it needed to succeed, both faced persistent criticism, and both were, perhaps prematurely, canceled.

DynaSoar

Before negotiations at the conclusion of World War II were complete, tensions between the Soviet Union and the United States – and ideological battles between communism and capitalism – were heating up. The Soviet Union's Joseph Stalin spoke of the incompatibility between the two systems, and in 1946, Britain's Winston Churchill declared that an "Iron Curtain" had descended across Europe. By 1949, the Soviet Union had tested its first atomic bomb, and Americans were in a panic. Knowledge of the Soviet's weapons capabilities was limited, and the U.S. was seeking opportunities to discover what weapons they had and what they were developing. The 1950s witnessed the Korean War, the split of Vietnam, and the communist takeover of Cuba. It was a time of massive military buildup and uncertainty.

By 1957, the space race between the Soviet Union and the United States was well underway. In October, when the Soviet Union launched the first artificial satellite, Sputnik 1, into an elliptical low earth orbit, the American public was shocked by the demonstrated lead of the Soviet space program. Terrified by the Soviet threat and unsure of their full capabilities, the U.S. government's need to do something new, something impressive, something indisputably superior became urgent. The fantasy of flying in space became the American imperative.

X-20 DynaSoar. Source: CSNR Reference Collection.

One avenue of potentially competitive technology was hypersonic flight. After conducting studies under the direction of the

Air Force spanning nearly two years, the Boeing Company began work on the DynaSoar ("Dynamic Soarer") program in November 1959. DynaSoar was an experimental piloted vehicle. The concept was a winged spaceplane, similar to the later Space Shuttle. DynaSoar was designed to be launched by a Titan booster, perform military missions in a suborbital trajectory, and glide back to earth in a controlled re-entry – the success of which was the main goal of the program. In late 1961, under the direction of the new Secretary of Defense Robert McNamara, officials reoriented DynaSoar. The spaceplane, re-designated the X-20, would now be launched into full orbit. The main objective of the program remained studying the maneuverability of re-entry from orbit, in addition to studying the sustainability of man in space.[1]

The MOL Concept and End of DynaSoar

In 1958, the Air Research and Development Command published a 275-page study titled, "Proposal for Man in Space;" the government was exploring an array of options for using man in space. The National Aeronautics and Space Administration (NASA) was established in July 1958 following a series of discussions and debates about what the United States space program should look like. Ultimately NASA was designed to be a completely unclassified, civilian, peaceful organization with goals of exploring space and maintaining the United States' technological supremacy. NASA immediately began work on a number of programs, including the manned Mercury program. However, NASA's nature prevented it from exploring military and reconnaissance capabilities in space. The Cold War was in full swing, and America needed to know more about the Soviet Union's capabilities. Although the government was actively using the U-2 spy plane by 1957, following the 1960 shoot-down of Gary Powers' aircraft, the U.S. was again blind to what was happening over the Iron Curtain; reconnaissance from space was the answer. NASA continued its programs, while the military pursued its own, creating opportunities for great collaboration, as well as tumultuous turf wars.

On 25 August 1962, while DynaSoar was still in development, Secretary of the Air Force Eugene Zuckert notified General Bernard Adolph Schriever, Commander of Air Force Systems Command and later MOL Director, that he was to proceed with studies of the Manned Orbiting Laboratory program.

Eugene M. Zuckert,
Secretary of the United States Air Force.
Source: CSNR Reference Collection.

Bernard A. Schriever.
Source: USAF.

Early MOL Model. Source: CSNR Reference Collection.

Although the Air Force was still studying and defining it, MOL was designed to be a laboratory launched into orbit, providing a facility for military astronauts to conduct a series of experiments, and then return to earth after a defined period of time. In addition to authorizing MOL in August 1962, Zuckert approved the selection of Douglas Aircraft Company as the laboratory associate contractor and the General Electric Company as the mission module associate contractor to help with the concept development and early MOL designs.[2]

Over the course of the next year, MOL proved to be a much more viable program than DynaSoar. Secretary of Defense McNamara, the President's Scientific Advisory Committee, and other government officials remained skeptical of the military usefulness, long-term goals, and necessity of DynaSoar, especially at such an expense. The lack of a long-term mission plagued the program, and even a 1961 redirection could not save DynaSoar. Remaining optimistic about the significance of a military man in space, on 10 December 1963, the Secretary of Defense, with President Lyndon Johnson's approval, publicly announced that he was terminating DynaSoar, and the Air Force was to pursue MOL in its stead. The original MOL concept was described as "an orbiting pressurized cylinder approximately the size of a small house trailer, [which] will increase the Defense Department effort to determine military usefulness of man in space."[3] In his statement to all major commands, Secretary McNamara explained, "In initiating the MOL program, it was decided to terminate the DYNASOAR (X-20) program because the current requirement is for a program aimed directly at the basic question of man's utility in space, rather than a program limited to finding means to control the return of man from space. The DYNASOAR Program was designed to do the latter."[4] Air Force efforts, resources, and a single DynaSoar pilot, Albert H. Crews, were transferred to the MOL program.

Early Studies

Following its initial authorization, MOL program officials spent the next 20 months conducting studies, hosting meetings, and refining concept designs and goals. In January 1964, the Air Force developed a strategy for initiating MOL. The plan was divided into Phases I, II, and III, with the early studies period underway labeled "Pre-phase I." The exact concept and scope of MOL was ambiguous and a work in progress.

Almost immediately upon announcement, MOL faced unrelenting scrutiny. Brigadier General John L. Martin, Jr., NRO Staff Director or, in the "white" (unclassified) world, Director of the Office of Space Systems, feared the publicity surrounding the highly-classified reconnaissance aspects of the program.[5] Following a conversation with Brig. Gen. Martin, in a memorandum to the Deputy Chief of Staff, R&D, dated 15 January 1964, Undersecretary of the Air Force and Director of the National Reconnaissance

John L. Martin.
Source: USAF.

Brockway McMillan.
Source: CSNR Reference Collection.

Office (DNRO) Brockway McMillan expressed unease regarding where the program office was placing its focus. McMillan was concerned that the program office was overemphasizing the role of man in space and the development of a manned reconnaissance system, while underemphasizing the experimental aspects of the program. McMillan warned, "It is absolutely crucial to the survival of this program that it be directed at the start to specified and fully approved objectives, and that it be held to these objectives until they are accomplished or changed. Development of a manned reconnaissance system is not an approved objective."[6] This was a reaction to the security concerns, however. Only weeks before DNRO McMillan's memorandum, on 3 December 1963, the NRO contracted with Eastman Kodak to study the value of manned and unmanned photo reconnaissance systems.[7] The potential for a spaceborne photoreconnaissance system remained central to the program and highly classified.

In the face of constant examination, the Preliminary MOL Technical Development Plan was completed in April 1964, and a number of studies were underway.[8] In total, the Air Force spent about $6 million on studies in an effort to determine the best use of and design for MOL, the majority of which were completed by the end of August 1964. In an effort to identify the necessary equipment and techniques for performing the primary MOL experiments, the Air Force contracted six separate Experiment Study Contracts. Similarly, six separate studies were conducted on the various major subsystems within MOL (environmental control, power, stabilization, guidance, communications, and possible radar). The Air Force contracted McDonnell Aircraft Corporation to study the Gemini B and potential interface issues with MOL, in addition to studying the utility of a modified one-man Gemini and its ability to perform MOL experiments. The Martin Marietta Corporation was signed to study the Titan III interfaces with MOL, and North American Aviation was contracted to study any potential Apollo applications.[9] In March of 1964, DNRO McMillan assigned NRO Program A Director, Major General Robert Evans Greer, to study the potential manned and unmanned satellite reconnaissance capabilities.[10]

Out of these studies, Harold Brown, the Director of Defense Research and Engineering (DDR&E) under Secretary of Defense McNamara (and later Secretary of Defense himself), argued that the two most promising uses of man in space were "the ability to recognize patterns and interpret them in real-time and report the results" as well as "the ability to point a sensor and provide image-motion

Harold R. Brown.
Source: CSNR Reference Collection.

Robert S. McNamara.
Source: CSNR Reference Collection.

compensation so that a very narrow field of view can encompass the area to be examined."[11] In response to the Gemini/MOL experiments, Colonel William Brady, MOL System Program Director, claimed in December 1964 that with MOL, the Air Force would be able to qualitatively and quantitatively measure the utility of a military man in space.[12] Although many would continue to scrutinize the utility of man in the MOL program, and in space in general, the studies were fruitful and the program was gaining momentum.

Armed with studies, support, and a general concept of what the program should accomplish, the Air Force distributed the MOL Request for Proposals (RFP's) to twenty contractors* in early January 1965.[13] By the end of February, the Air Force had selected four contractors for the MOL preliminary design studies: the Boeing Company, Douglas Aircraft Company, Inc., General Electric Company, and Lockheed Corporation.[14] The design was far from complete and the program was yet to receive official presidential sanction, but the work was underway.

MOL Experiments

With the cancellation of DynaSoar still fresh for many, it was essential that MOL define clear, attainable, long-term, and justifiable goals. But a consensus among those involved was difficult to achieve. Between February and July 1965, officials confirmed the main objective of the program to be the development of an operationally useful high resolution manned photoreconnaissance program.[15] But officials still debated the most effective use of military man in space, and even those who supported the photoreconnaissance program from the beginning were wary of security concerns, forcing MOL officials to present other "white" program objectives. One of the most attractive opportunities with MOL was the ability for man to conduct experiments in space, for man to be able to grasp and quantify what he could do in space, and how he could contribute to

---

* The Boeing Company, Chrysler Corporation, Douglas Aircraft Company, Inc., General Dynamics Corporation, General Electric Company, Goodyear Aircraft Corporation, Grumman Aircraft Engineering Corporation, Hughes Aircraft Company, Ling Temco Vought, Inc., Lockheed Corporation, Martin Company, McDonnell Aircraft Corporation, North American Aviation Corporation, Northrop Corporation, Radio Corporation of America, Raytheon Company, Republic Aviation Corporation, TRW Space Technology Labs, United Aircraft Corporation, Western Electric Company, Inc.

national defense from orbit. From 27-28 February 1964, the MOL Technical Panel held its first meeting at the Naval Research Laboratory (NRL) under the chairmanship of NRL's Dr. W. C. Hall. The group received 89 experiment proposals or topic ideas for Navy astronautic systems alone.[16] Over time, the group continued to carefully consider and weigh each potential experiment. A month after that initial meeting, on 26 March 1964, DNRO McMillan established guidelines for the experiments – they were to explore the possible contribution of man, security was to be strict, and the potential of the manned and unmanned systems were to be explored and compared.[17]

> *"...putting man in the position of a pointer not a thinker..."*

MOL leadership hotly debated what types of experiments were to be included in the program. A preliminary list of MOL experiments was viciously criticized by some, arguing that the program needed to be modified immediately, "Otherwise we just finished planning DYNASOAR II."[18] Criticisms included that the initial plan degraded the role of the astronaut, putting man in the position of "a pointer not a thinker;" that the role of man in MOL would quickly be replaced by machine; and that there needed to be greater emphasis on bioastronautics experiments, engineering technology, and system experiments.[19] In the midst of discussion and debate, Albert C. Hall, in his role as deputy for space technology, Office of the Director, Defense Research and Engineering, proposed a division between two kinds of experiments, those regarding observation and those regarding subsystems and bioastronautics.[20] The observational experiments included studying the ability of man to detect and track a ground target; to reach conclusions from events and report to earth; to process film already exposed, detect significant information, and then report that data back to earth; and to observe and classify ships at sea, as well as other space vehicles. In contrast, the subsystem and bioastronautics experiments included monitoring the feedback of human performance in space and working to enhance the ability of man to perform military missions effectively in the space environment.[21]

In April 1964, the Manned Orbiting Laboratory Experiments Working Group published a 499-page document detailing all proposed experiments and descriptions – everything was being considered. In July 1964, DNRO McMillan suggested considering man's role in erecting large antennas in space. In a memorandum to Colonel Schultz, a MOL program official, DNRO McMillan explained, "One advantage of the benign space environment is that a very large antenna could be supported by a light structure, provided it could be erected and adjusted. Man's best contribution might be in erecting and adjusting such an antenna outside a vehicle in orbit. Both the value of such an antenna to the electromagnetic mission, and the feasibility of managing its construction, must be considered as the MOL program takes shape."[22] The value of such antennas would be immeasurable to future NRO signals intelligence (sigint) missions. After extensive discussion and debate, the working group narrowed down the experiments to a final 13 primary experiments in March 1965. These primary experiments all focused on measuring the utility of man in space. Several secondary experiments were to be included as well, focused on advancing technology or providing scientific data of unusual importance.[23]

MOL's Proponents and Critics

From late 1964 through the first half of 1965, government officials continued to clarify the need for MOL and what it should accomplish. In August 1964, Alexander Flax, Assistant Secretary of the Air Force for Research and Development, sent a memorandum to his Deputy Chief of Staff emphasizing the importance of MOL. At that time, the tentative schedule called for the first unmanned MOL launch during the 1968 calendar year. Flax felt the program was more urgent than that and argued,

"The importance of the MOL program dictates that the Air Force investigate alternatives for shortening the development cycle."[24] MOL had another staunch supporter in General Schriever. In June 1965, he wrote a letter to General John Paul McConnell, the Air Force Chief of Staff, in which he argued, "I am sure you agree that this program is of unparalleled importance to the Air Force and that every action must be taken which will contribute to its success."[25] He agreed that the task at hand was complex and reasoned that the program "will demand the very best talent and experience in the industry."[26]

Although many saw the need and potential for the MOL program, the Air Force was still sorting out what it would accomplish. In a January 1965 memorandum from DDR&E Harold Brown to the Under Secretary of the Air Force, Brown explained, "The Secretary of Defense has changed the priority of the objectives of the MOL program to provide more emphasis to developments that may lead to operational systems."[27] This reorganization of goals meant that the first priority of the program was now to develop "technology contributing to improved military observational capability for manned or unmanned operation" followed by developing and demonstrating "manned assembly and service of large structures in orbit with potential military applications."[28] The third objective allowed for more flexibility and was to provide for "other manned military experimentation."[29] According to many, MOL was a critical military program that would allow for essential military reconnaissance from space.

Alexander H. Flax.
Source: CSNR Reference Collection.

However, even with an impressive experiment plan and ambitious set of goals outlined, many remained skeptical of MOL. One of the most debated advantages of the MOL program was the increased resolution of reconnaissance photographs dubbed Very High Resolution (VHR).[30] The U.S. was flying and developing several satellite photoreconnaissance programs at this point; the question was whether or not MOL could add significant value. The first satellite reconnaissance imagery was collected from the Corona system in August 1960. Corona flew the KH-4 camera in 1962 and 1963, achieving ground resolution in the seven to nine-foot range. Corona's intelligence answered many pressing questions regarding Soviet capabilities and weaponry build-up. But its resolution was limiting. By late 1966, the newly-created NRO began flying Gambit, a satellite with two to three-foot resolution – a vast improvement over Corona. However, as automated systems, both Corona and Gambit were limited in their ability to react to real-time situations. Similarly, both systems deployed their film capsules, which the Air Force then recovered mid-air. Given the capsule return and film processing times, turnaround from the time of photography to when the film was prepared for analysis was a matter of weeks – a significant delay during a time of crisis, as proven by the disastrous 1961 Bay of Pigs invasion.

The initial plans for MOL claimed that it would provide reconnaissance photography with at least superior resolution, an improvement over both the Corona and Gambit systems. While some argued that this increase in resolution was absolutely essential to monitoring arms agreements and maintaining dominance during the Cold War, others disagreed. In January 1965, the President's Scientific Advisory Committee (PSAC) downplayed the significance of MOL's promise and stated that an increase in performance from the current high resolution to the promised superior resolution was insufficient to warrant the manned system.[31] Instead, the PSAC argued that the only way to justify a manned system was to approach the atmospheric limit.[32]

In June 1965, the President's Scientific Advisor, Dr. Donald Hornig, weighed in on MOL. In a memorandum addressed to the Secretary of Defense, Dr. Hornig expressed both approval and concern over the program.[33] While he acknowledged that the VHR imagery provided by MOL would undoubtedly be helpful to the nation's intelligence and defense communities, Hornig also acknowledged that there were other pressing intelligence concerns which would not be met by MOL.

The major obstacle for Hornig was MOL's use of man. On one hand, he argued that the Air Force proved that man was essential to attaining the products the MOL program promised. Hornig articulated, "With regard to the MOL proposal itself, the Air Force has done an exceedingly thorough analysis of both the manned and unmanned system alternatives for a high resolution optical reconnaissance system. It has, in my opinion, documented a persuasive argument that, for equal total weights and total volumes, the manned system does have an advantage over the unmanned system and can be expected to provide a higher average resolution at an earlier time than the unmanned system."[34] However, Hornig feared the political fallout of a manned system, a concern for many involved in the early development of the program. He claimed, "I believe that very serious political questions [will] arise from the MOL program."[35] Weighing both sides of the argument, Hornig recommended that the President approve the MOL program, but concurrently develop an unmanned capability for the system. In a separate memorandum to the President from the same date, Hornig warned that the President must prepare to assume serious political risks.[36] Dr. Hornig acknowledged the importance of the MOL mission, but also realized that the proposed MOL program was riddled with risks. Plowing ahead, on 28 June 1965, eighteen months of Air Force studies, analyses, and back-and-forth efforts culminated in a 14-page Air Force memorandum for the proposed MOL program.[37] The proposal was approved by the Air Force and forwarded to the Office of the Secretary of Defense (OSD).

Donald F. Hornig.
Source: CSNR Reference Collection.

MOL and the Public

In the spring and summer of 1965, as the possibility of presidential approval and public announcement became more of a reality and the circle of those briefed on the program expanded, MOL proponents faced two major hurdles: program security and the potentially negative international reaction to MOL. In May 1965, the NRO Chief Security Officer, Louis F. Mazza, drafted a memorandum to MOL officials Brigadier General James T. Stewart and Brigadier General Harry L. Evans outlining the security problems related to MOL.[38] First and foremost, despite its classified and unapproved status, the MOL program had already received considerable press coverage identifying its primary mission as reconnaissance, and there was no good way to refute such claims. Mazza explained, "The problem of the press must be examined recognizing that there exists no conceivable 'cover' for the MOL reconnaissance mission. We are forced to rely completely upon a system of rigid security."[39] The existence of such press coverage proved that this "system of rigid security" was not going to work.

As an alternative, Mazza suggested a plan to reorient the program away from black (covert) and white (open) experiments and instead focus on stated program objectives. In his memorandum, Mazza laid out his plan: "Admit we have a DoD [Department of Defense] manned orbital laboratory and its mission is to determine man's potential usefulness in space. Do not try to build the MOL in a completely covert atmosphere. Do not try to launch the MOL under a covert condition. Do not try to control all activities under BYEMAN or clear all participants Dorian."[40] Rather than trying to protect a secret which was proving impossible to keep under wraps or provide a cover for something that was already being questioned, Mazza proposed a hybrid program which would be announced publicly and have an open mission, and yet maintain a covert reconnaissance objective, similar to the Discoverer/Corona program.

Concern over public knowledge and how to handle the program had been in discussion across government organizations for well over a year. In March 1964, Deputy Assistant Secretary of State for Politico-Military Affairs Jeffrey C. Kitchen wrote a letter to Assistant Secretary of Defense for International Security Affairs John T. McNaughton to address his concerns. Kitchen stated, "In view of the fact that a good deal of information about the MOL has already been made public through Congressional hearings and public statements, it would clearly not be reasonable to expect that the general characteristics, purpose, and success or failure of its launches will not be made public. I am, therefore, inclined to believe that most aspects of the MOL program will have to be conducted with reasonable openness. At the same time, there may be aspects which it would be preferable to put under specific restraints. In short, I believe the MOL program requires specific guidelines of its own for public affairs handling and in turn may pose particular foreign policy issues."[41]

MOL on the International Stage

Pursuing this hybrid and somewhat open approach, once the MOL program was announced, officials feared how it would be received internationally. On 8 July 1965, Spurgeon M. Keeny, Jr., a senior staff member on the National Security Council under McGeorge Bundy, United States National Security Advisor, wrote a memorandum to the Vice President articulating his concern over MOL. Keeny argued, "The MOL project was introduced by Secretary McNamara as a substitute for DYNASOAR to explore the possible military use of space and has been widely associated by the technical press with a wide range of military systems including reconnaissance and weapons delivery. Therefore, despite the growing tacit acceptance of unmanned satellite reconnaissance, there is certainly a danger that

William F. Raborn, Jr..
Source: CSNR Reference Collection.

David Dean Rusk.
Source: CSNR Reference Collection.

the Soviets will consider MOL to be a military overflight of their country and will either demand that such flights not be undertaken or will use this as a pretext for a demand that we stop our entire reconnaissance program."[42] Although Keeny admitted that he may have been exaggerating the problem, it was certainly a possibility worth consideration.

On 9 July 1965, Secretary of Defense McNamara presented the MOL concept to Dr. Glenn Seaborg, Chairman of the United States Atomic Energy Commission; James Webb, NASA Administrator; Secretary of State Dean Rusk; and Vice Admiral William Raborn, Director of the CIA. During the meeting, Secretary Rusk voiced concern over MOL's international reception, and NASA requested a policy regarding MOL's approved status. In response, Secretary McNamara agreed to prepare a "posture" paper – a task he delegated to Dr. Brown which was then passed to Dr. Hall and eventually wound up on the desk of Colonel Paul E. Worthman of the NRO staff.[43] By mid-July, Colonel Worthman drafted a MOL policy which, building on Krushchev's comments from 1960 that he would not be opposed to overflight, "advocates a conservative approach to MOL security and publicity."[44]

This "Policy on Public Information Aspects and International Reactions to the MOL" or "MOL Posture Paper," completed at the end of July, was the first MOL Policy and served as the template for the public presentation of MOL. Although officials recognized that some public presentation of the program was necessary, the policy concluded that "disclosure of the MOL reconnaissance capability is an irreversible step which would have profound adverse effects on enemies, allies, and neutrals. Furthermore, no gain would appear to flow from disclosure."[45] The paper argued that the U.S. must resist the suggestion that MOL requires elaborate justification, and instead keep the public information modest. The policy stated that the public announcement of MOL must treat the program as an investigation and development of manned orbital capabilities, not reconnaissance, while reaffirming the United States' abhorrence of orbiting weapons. Although public announcement was to avoid using the word "reconnaissance" directly, using "observation" or "photographic" in its stead, hope remained that the program would lay the groundwork for the acceptance of reconnaissance. According to the policy, program security would be tight, the program's status and effectiveness would not be discussed, and the program would be described as under the stewardship of the DoD. Although information on program specifics was highly classified, and policy stated that the U.S. would avoid the question of the program's legitimacy altogether, it did allow that selected information could be discretely shared with allies. Regardless of what was publicly announced, however, the policy made clear that, "the classified military objectives will continue to have top priority and no steps should be taken to use any possible NASA interests as a cover."[46]

As more and more people were briefed into the program, more and more people wanted to study issues. Also a result of the 9 July meeting, the CIA's VADM Raborn "instructed the appropriate committee of the United States Intelligence Board (USIB) to examine the intelligence requirements for very high resolution photography of the character envisaged for acquisition by the Manned Orbiting Laboratory (MOL)."[47] This, however, presented a number of challenges and a slow-down in the process. By the end of July, Dr. Hall asked Col Worthman to draft a document to USIB requesting their support for MOL and expressing a desire for USIB to get out of program specifics.[48]

Concern over international push-back continued until the program was announced. In a letter to Secretary of Defense McNamara from mid-August 1965, Secretary of State Rusk reiterated his concerns and stated that although the U.S. was likely to encounter international problems if MOL was carried out as planned, he was not advising against it. Instead, he emphasized the need for tight control of the program and any publicity, as well as strict avoidance of any statements indicating military implications or future potential.

MOL Takes Shape

By early August 1965, officials had agreed upon most of the details of the proposed program. In a memorandum to President Johnson dated 10 August 1965, Secretary McNamara outlined the program and gave his recommendations.[49] With a price tag of $1.5 billion, the proposed program would include six initial launches, one unmanned and five manned, each mission lasting 30 days, with the possibility to extend over time. MOL was scheduled to launch into polar orbit from the Western Test Range at Vandenberg Air Force Base in California using a modified Titan IIIC booster.[50] Larry Glass, a former engineer on the MOL program, explained that the modified Titan was designed to have "seven segments in the solids instead of five, the upper stage was replaced with a longer-stage that was really the laboratory. On top of that was a modified Gemini capsule" in which the astronauts would launch into space and return to earth at the completion of their mission.[51]

MOL's objectives were primarily "to secure photographs of [superior] resolutions of significant targets," to develop "high-resolution optical technology and systems for either manned or unmanned use," to provide "a facility for the development, test and use of other potential military applications,"

Early drawing of the MOL concept. Source: CSNR Reference Collection.

Gemini capsule.
Source: CSNR Reference Collection.

In The Words of Those Who Served

and to offer "an experimental program for determination of man's utility in assembling large structures, and in adjusting, maintaining and processing the output from complex military equipment in space."[52] Working toward those objectives, McNamara reinforced the necessity of security to prevent international concerns, keeping public information modest and low key.

There was a significant amount of work to be done and a number of contractors to help accomplish it all. Martin Marietta was selected to integrate the booster; United Technology Center was selected as the associate contractor for the solid rocket motors; McDonnell Aircraft Corporation was contracted to produce the Gemini spacecraft; and Aerospace Corporation was selected to provide system engineering and technical direction for the Air Force.[53]

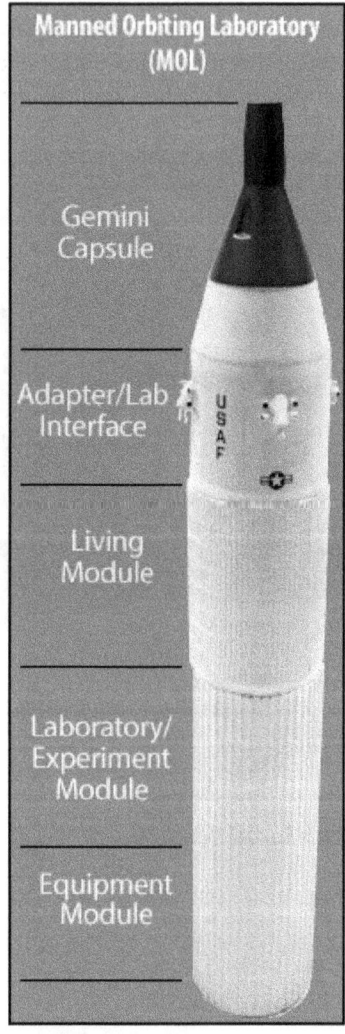

Above: MOL configuration diagram.
Source: CSNR Reference Collection.

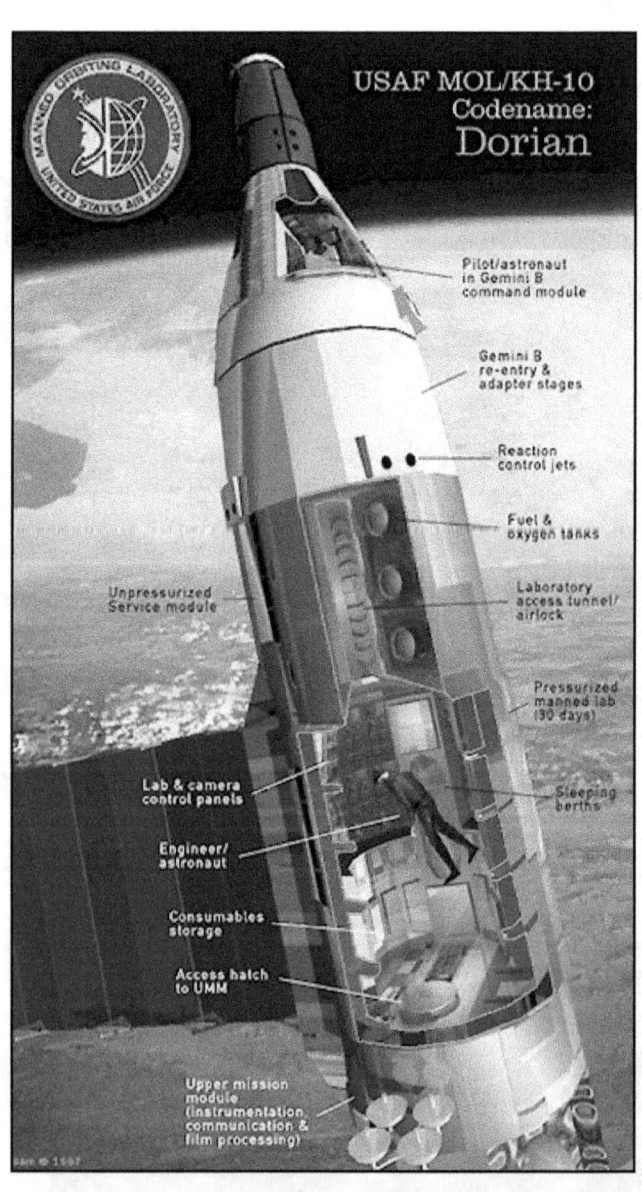

Above: Dorian diagram.
Source: CSNR Reference Collection.

Even with a plan in place, McNamara acknowledged that the program still lacked universal support. Despite criticism from the Director of the Bureau of Budget that the manned program was not worth the cost and risk, McNamara recommended that the President approve the full-scale development of MOL in fiscal year (FY) 1966. He stated, "I believe that there is a vital national need for reconnaissance photography at a resolution of [superior] or better," arguing that it would be used for improved technical intelligence, in times of crisis, and in better policing arms control agreements. Likewise, the improved resolution would undoubtedly provide the U.S. with a better assessment of Soviet and Chinese capabilities and technology. McNamara concluded, "My judgment is that we should now proceed to acquire the benefits of an experimental manned system."[54]

The Program Office

But how would this new hybrid program be run? How would a publicly acknowledged program with covert objectives be structured? By early 1964, government officials were already engaged in debate on this topic. In a letter to General Schriever in February 1964, DNRO McMillan suggested that MOL maintain offices in Washington, D.C., which would manage the high-level program concerns: developing and maintaining the experimental plan, coordinating plans with NASA, ensuring support from all elements of the Air Force Systems Command, managing the budget, monitoring progress, and providing timely information to the Secretary of the Air Force, Air Staff, and Deputy Director of Research and Development. In that vein, McMillan stated, "I favor the appointment of a special assistant to the Secretary of the Air Force who would assist the Secretary in the review of the progress of the program. The assistant would be continuously informed of actions taken by the MOL office and by the Air Staff, and of the status of relations with the NASA."[55] McMillan did acknowledge the complexity of the issue, however, and suggested that the relationship of MOL to other programs remained problematic, and it would have to be detached but coordinated enough to prevent competition for resources and duplicative efforts.

Officials continued to study the issue and, in July 1965, Brigadier General Evans presented a plan to DNRO McMillan and General Schriever, explaining, "In summary, the attached paper provides for a strong, autonomous integrated program implementation office located at SSD/Aerospace, headed by a general officer. It provides strong centralized integrated total program direction from a Washington area office, reporting directly to SAF/SAFUS/DNRO. This office would be headed by General B.A. Schriever as Director, MOL, as an additional duty. He would be supported by: (1) a full-time Vice Director and staff located in the Washington area; (2) the MOL Advisory Committee formed by the NAS."[56] Brig. Gen. Evans' plan was generally accepted and solidified in the Management of the MOL Program directive No. 65-1.[57] Effective 24 August 1965, the day before MOL was publicly announced, General Schriever was designated Director of the MOL office.[58] The debate over the structure of the program and who was responsible for what tasks, however, was far from over.

MOL Goes Public

On 25 August 1965, President Johnson publicly announced the approved MOL program. The month prior was filled with the back-and-forth debate over what should be announced and how questions should be answered. Colonel Worthman, having drafted the MOL public policy paper, drafted both the initial press release, as well as responses to anticipated press questions.[59]

On 27 July 1965, Colonel Worthman provided two separate answers for three questions, one set of classified answers for the Space Council and one set of answers for the public. Addressing the question of whether or not MOL was changing the peaceful nature of the U.S.'s current manned space program, the short answer for both was "No." To the Space Council, it was recommended to highlight that public information would be limited and deliberate and that the U.S. maintains commitment to its opposition to orbiting weapons. To the public, the emphasis was placed on the fact that MOL was an investigation and development of manned orbital capabilities for national defense. More succinctly, "It would be noted that MOL is a laboratory."[60] Anticipating concerns over why the program would be launched from the Western Test Range, for both the Space Council and the public, the answer was simply that launches were to be held on both U.S. coasts, but that launching into near-polar orbits from the Western Test Range would allow collection of flight data from all space regions. Lastly, the biggest anticipated concern remained the perception by the international community that MOL maintained a secretly aggressive agenda. To both audiences, the answer remained that the U.S. joined the United Nations (UN) in adopting a resolution against orbiting weapons and that the U.S. would not deviate in their support.

The proposed press release was reviewed and edited by a number of government officials, including Dr. Hall, Dr. McMillan, and Secretary of Defense McNamara. In the end, President Johnson delivered a concise statement, opening a televised White House press conference. Johnson announced the cost of the program, tentative schedule, and contractors. Avoiding any discussion of reconnaissance, Johnson announced, "This program will bring us new knowledge about what man is able to do in space. It will enable us to relate that ability to the defense of America. It will develop technology and equipment which will help advance manned and unmanned space flights. And it will make it possible to perform their new and rewarding experiments with that technology and equipment."[61] MOL was indeed designed to accomplish all that – and so much more.

Establishing a Program Office

Government officials had been working for well over a year to establish a program structure to meet the unique needs of the MOL program. Following the President's announcement of the MOL program, Air Force officials revealed the names of MOL leadership on 30 August 1965. General Bernard A. Schriever, commander of the newly-created Air Force Systems Command, had been leading MOL development since December 1963 and was assigned additional duties as the Director of MOL. Located in Washington, D.C., General Schriever reported directly to the Secretary of the Air Force.[62] General Schriever's Vice Director was Brigadier General Harry Evans, moving over from the Office of the Joint Chiefs of Staff, also located in Washington. Brig. Gen. Evans was responsible for MOL's Program Office at the Pentagon. [63] Schriever's Deputy Director, who headed the MOL offices at the Air Force Space Systems Division in El Segundo, California, was Brigadier General Russell A. Berg who had been serving as Deputy Director for Special Projects in Los Angeles at the time.[64]

Russell A. Berg. Source: USAF.

Ultimately, the Secretary of the Air Force provided the policy, guidance, and final Air Force approval for the program.[65] The Director of MOL and the Secretary of the Air Force provided program guidance, while the Deputy Director of MOL facilitated program implementation.[66] But the MOL program posed unique management issues in that the program was operating in the

John S. Foster, Jr..
Source: CSNR Reference Collection.

Joseph S. Bleymaier.
Source: USAF.

open "white" world, but maintained a highly-classified "black" mission. On the outside, MOL was an experimental orbiting laboratory run by the Air Force. But under the surface, the reconnaissance mission – codenamed Dorian in the BYEMAN security system – was at the heart of the program. One procedural document explained, "MOL represented a unique management problem, broad in both scope and complexity with a program structure quite different from that of previous satellite reconnaissance programs."[67]

By September, officials began sorting out a management approach for the hybrid program, and a number of agreements were discussed and signed. General Schriever and Brig. Gen. John Martin, Director of the Secretary of the Air Force Office of Special Projects (SAFSP), signed an agreement stating that both the Director of SAFSP and the Director of MOL would enjoy essentially the same level of "responsibility, authority, and managerial latitude" for their respective parts of MOL.[68] Given the security considerations, many of the more sensitive aspects of the program such as "black" contracting would be managed under the Director of SAFSP in the Sensor Payload Office. On the other hand, the Deputy Director of MOL would handle the "white" aspects of the mission such as mission planning. With offices split between Washington, D.C. and California, General Schriever and Brig. Gen. Martin agreed that as much of the work as possible would be delegated to California, while only issues that needed to be handled in Washington, D.C. would be managed there.

As officials were establishing the program office, several major Air Force and defense players transitioned. DNRO McMillan left the NRO on 30 September 1965, succeeded by Alexander Flax as DNRO, in addition to his responsibilities as Assistant Secretary of the Air Force (R&D). On 1 October 1965, Dr. Harold Brown succeeded Eugene M. Zuckert as Secretary of the Air Force. With Harold Brown's DDR&E position now vacant, Dr. John S. Foster, Jr. stepped in to fill the role. In response to these changes, General Schriever and the new DNRO Flax signed an agreement similar to the Schriever/Martin agreement of September 1965, concluding that MOL was subject to the DNRO as an element of the National Reconnaissance Program (NRP) with respect to its imaging and proposed but, unexplored, sigint capabilities. Essentially, DNRO Flax had authority over the MOL reconnaissance payloads.[69] However, due to the critical role of man in the program, the Secretary of the Air Force, "with the advice and assistance of the DNRO, [was] responsible for executive management of all aspects of MOL."[70] Given security concerns between the "white" and "black" elements of the program, the DDR&E, a position now filled by Dr. Foster, was a bridge between the two worlds.[71] Other key players in MOL program management were Major General Ben I. Funk, Commander of the Air Force's Space Systems Division, and Brigadier General Joseph S. Bleymaier, recently assigned Commander of the Western Test Range.[72]

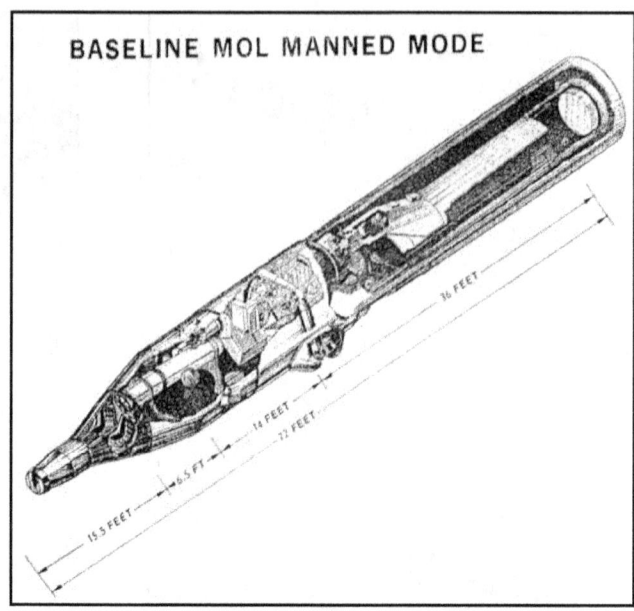

MOL diagram.
Source: CSNR Reference Collection.

Although agreements were reached early, these divisions were messy, and disagreements plagued the management office. Shortly after the initial agreement was signed between General Schriever and Brig. Gen. Martin, Colonel Worthman summarized the situation in a memorandum by stating the generals' positions as, "General Evans: 'If I'm running the MOL Program, I expect to run all parts of it and to direct all participants.' General Martin: 'The Dorian Program is run by the Director, NRO. My guidance and direction comes solely from him.'" Colonel Worthman went on to note, "These differences are fundamental and may be irresolvable." Given the centrality of man's role in MOL, General Schriever felt that he, as Director of MOL, should be heavily involved in the development of the MOL payload. Due to strict security, however, Brig. Gen. Martin maintained that the NRO was the ultimate authority on the payload. Though General Schriever and his deputy Brig. Gen. Evans were displeased, the program continued to operate under those compromises until the program entered the engineering phase of development. [73]

The Mechanics of MOL

With both presidential approval and a program office in place, work on MOL was noticeably progressing by late 1965. Over the next year, "MOL activities focused on detailed program definition, the selection of major subcontractors, and contract negotiations."[74] The MOL design was divided into segments based on utility during the mission. The Gemini B was designed to provide crew support, protection, and transportation. The laboratory module, at 10 feet in diameter and 19 feet long, was designed as crew and mission support during the orbital flight phase. The module contained a 1,000-cubic foot pressurized compartment which would allow for a shirt-sleeve working environment for the two-man crew during its 30-day mission. The Mission Payload System Segment (MPSS) was designed as the photographic system and subsystems necessary for control and dynamics. It was an unpressurized module 10 feet in diameter and 37 feet long.[75] The photographic system, a large focal length camera-optical system with a 70-inch aperture, was designed to be capable of providing at least superior resolution photographs from an altitude of 80 nautical miles.[76] In 1969, the Dorian camera system was designated KH-10 within the Talent-Keyhole community.[77] After the lab

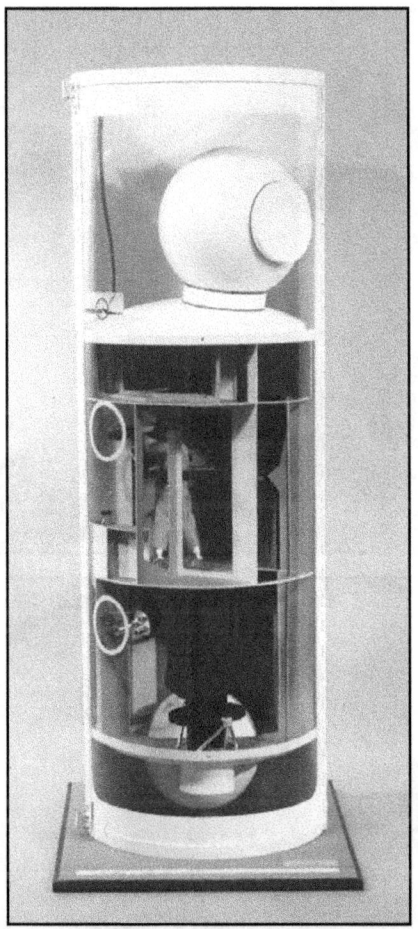

MOL model.
Source: CSNR Reference Collection.

MOL test flight 3 November 1966.
Source: CSNR Reference Collection.

module was tested, it would be mated with the mission module at the lab vehicle contractor's plant in order to form the complete lab vehicle. Together, they would be transported to the launch site and mated with the Titan IIIM and Gemini B.[78]

The vision for MOL was that the Gemini B, mission module, and laboratory module integrated unit would be launched from Vandenberg Air Force Base by a Titan IIIM (modified Titan IIIC) into an 80 X 186nm elliptical orbit.[79] On-orbit command and control was to be exercised through the Air Force Satellite Control Facility (SCF) at Sunnyvale Air Force Station in California.[80] During the early orbit phase of up to three earth orbits, the crew would check all systems and attain stabilized orbit.[81] Once stable orbit was achieved, one crew member would climb from the Gemini capsule into the laboratory module via a hatch cut in the heat shield of the Gemini capsule, while the other stayed in the Gemini B in order to prepare it for its 30-day standby mode. Once both crewmen had successfully completed their tasks, the second crewman would transfer to the lab module via the same tunnel.[82] Robert Crippen, a crew member selected for MOL in 1966, explained, "We had taken a regular Gemini that NASA had designed and was flying, and [we] cut a hatch in the ablative heat shield that protects you on the re-entry. There was some concern as to whether that would cause the shield not to be able to do its job, so there was a test flight that was flown to go check that out."[83] A successful test on 3 November 1966 demonstrated

17

In The Words of Those Who Served

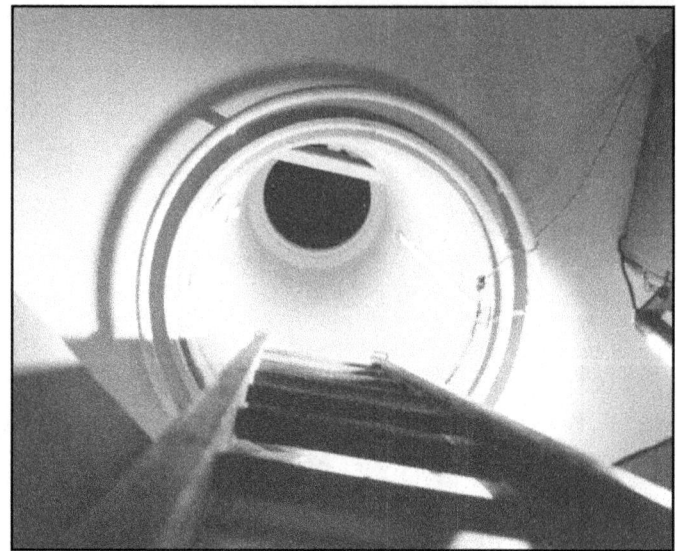

Tunnel connecting the laboratory module and Gemini capsule.
Source: CSNR Reference Collection.

MOL laboratory.
Source: CSNR Reference Collection.

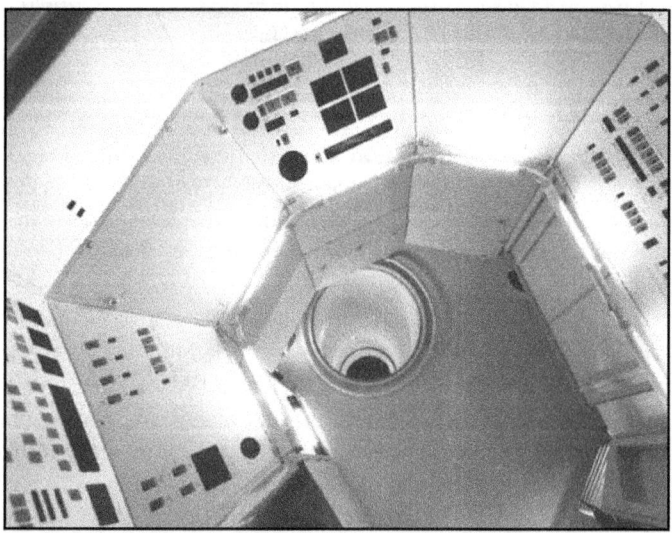

Tunnel returning to Gemini capsule from laboratory.
Source: CSNR Reference Collection.

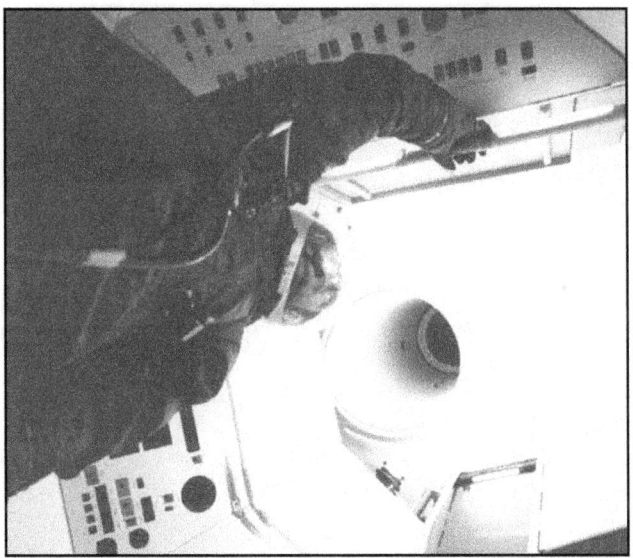

MOL tunnel. Source: CSNR Reference Collection.

that the heat shield,† with the hatch cut in it for crew access, was indeed able to withstand reentry.[84]

Once in the laboratory, the crew members would spend their 30-day mission working in a shirt-sleeve environment, acquiring very high resolution photography of the Soviet Union and other targets as needed, and participating in various experiments. DNRO Flax stated in 1966, "The only approved and funded mission of the MOL program is that of very high resolution optical photographic reconnaissance in support of National Reconnaissance Program objectives."[85] Vice Admiral Richard Truly, one of the first MOL crew members selected, described the mission as "a 30-day reconnaissance mission in a polar orbit for strategic image intelligence of the Soviet Union." He went on to explain that the majority of the targets were "the Soviet space program and missile program and aviation program."[86] Crew members were expected to have access to targets north of the 30th parallel (most of the Soviet Union) at least four times a day. Accounting for potential cloud cover, officials expected crew members to be able to photograph a minimum of 1500 cloud-free targets per 30-day mission.[87]

Upon completion of the mission, the crew would climb back into the Gemini capsule, detach from the laboratory, and return to earth in the Gemini; the MOL hardware remaining in space became refuse. Lachlan Macleay, one of the first crew members selected, recalled, "The question that really got us, and I think really Dick Helms said, 'After you come back in the Gemini capsule, what happens to the equipment?' They'd say, 'It gets dumped in the ocean.' That was kind of a downer. The system wasn't designed so you could rendezvous and put another crew in it. It was a one-shot 30-day thing. And that was a big deal in those days because a lot of the doctors weren't sure what the hell would happen to you in 30 days."[88]

After landing at a pre-designated landing area in either the Pacific or Atlantic oceans, the DoD air and sea forces used for the Apollo program would recover the capsule and crew members.[89] Although the MOL plan called for a water landing for the Gemini capsule, Air Force crews would also need to be on standby in case of emergency and early return to earth. In late 1966, the State Department began coordinating with the Chilean embassy in order to use Easter Island as an aircraft staging area for the MOL recovery forces.[90] After much time and diplomatic negotiation, an agreement was reached on 26 July 1968 that allowed the U.S. Air Force to conduct search and rescue operations from an Easter Island base.[91] Additional forces would be stationed around the world in case of contingency situations with return to earth or abort from powered flight.[92]

---

† The tested Gemini B capsule is on display at the National Museum of the United States Air Force located at Wright-Patterson Air Force Base outside Dayton, Ohio.

In The Words of Those Who Served

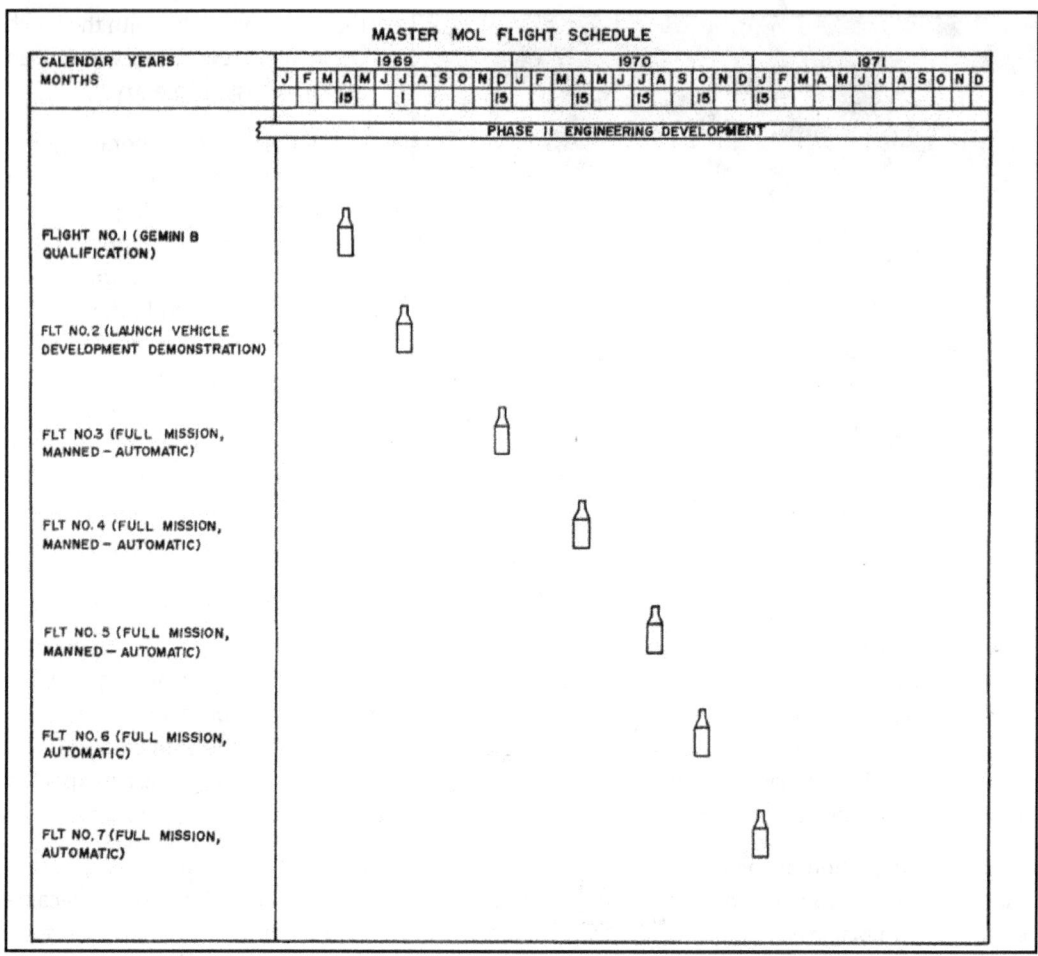

Master flight schedule as of 1 September 1966. Source: NROARC.

By October 1965, eight crew members had been selected, and a plan was in place to select twelve more. The MOL plan now called for seven initial flights, up from the original six. MOL flight 1 was scheduled to fly the Titan IIIC system, a simulated laboratory, and either a simulated or used Gemini capsule in March 1968. The flight was to be unmanned, and the mission objective was to qualify the system. The second flight, scheduled for July 1968, was planned as another unmanned flight of the Titan IIIC, the laboratory structure, and a Gemini B capsule. That flight would demonstrate the integrity of the Gemini B subsystem, the laboratory vehicle, and the flight and re-entry capability of the system. The first manned flight, MOL 3, was scheduled to fly in November 1968. MOL 3 was scheduled to be a shorter flight than a full-up manned flight, but it would demonstrate and verify the complete system, while crew members confirmed their ability to transfer to the laboratory module and conduct a series of biomedical and human performance tests. MOL flights 4 through 7, estimated to fly about four months apart, were all scheduled to be full 30-day duration, manned flights.[93] Flights 6 and 7 were later reevaluated and proposed to be unmanned flights.[94] In the unmanned configuration, engineers would remove the components and subsystems required for man, replace the Gemini B with the support module, and add the necessary unique components to enable the lab vehicle to interface with the added support module.[95] The flight schedule was continually evaluated and adjusted, slipping more than a year by the time the second group of MOL astronauts reported for duty in September 1966.

Government officials debated the role of the MOL crew members over the entire life of the program, forcing a dual-design for the program. In the manned version, renamed the "manned-automatic" version, the equipment would be operated automatically under the crew's supervision, allowing for manual override capability.[96] However, many critics remained proponents of the unmanned or "automatic" version throughout the program's existence. According to the January 1966 design requirements, each MOL vehicle would be designed in a manner that allowed for conversion to complete unmanned operation up to four months before launch, allowing for maximum flexibility.[97] For many, man in space was what made the MOL program unique and essential. Admiral Truly explained, "The idea was humans could help pick targets in real time, they could identify cloud cover and save film. The system was resource-limited because it was a film system, not electronic like we have now. But the whole idea was to have a far more capable intelligence capability because you had people there that could think and act and take action in real time during the flight."[98] The debate over the role of man, like so many other disagreements in the program, was far from over.

With early focus on establishing a program plan and the reconnaissance capabilities of the program, the MOL Policy Committee observed, "Presently no work is going on in establishing firm experimental objectives in the technological and scientific area, and only a limited amount of emphasis is being laid upon experimental objectives in the primary and secondary areas."[99] In a letter to Brig. Gen. Berg, Brig. Gen. Evans observed that although MOL had accomplished much in 1965, the program should be broadened beyond the scope of reconnaissance, writing that "it seems risky to make a prior determination that there is nothing of military significance in space other than reconnaissance."[100] Brig. Gen. Berg stated that they needed to "increase [MOL's] capabilities to perform useful military functions and experiments in space" and recommended that they "improve our organization and our capabilities to fulfill these broader objectives."[101] MOL continually evolved over the course of the program in order to meet the needs and criticisms of an ever-changing environment.

MOL Contractors

On 23 January 1965, the Secretary of Defense announced that they were issuing a Request for Proposals (RFP) from industry for design studies for the upcoming MOL program. By March, four contractors had been chosen from the original seven – Boeing Company, General Electric Company, Douglas Aircraft Company, and Lockheed Corporation.[102] The program was presidentially approved in August of that year, and by 1966, work was well under way.

Rather than contract the entire MOL program to one company, pieces of the program were contracted out to the company with capabilities that best fit each requirement. Contracts were negotiated in 1966 and 1967; the Aerospace Corporation was to conduct the general systems engineering and provide technical direction, the Martin Marietta Corporation was to provide the Titan IIIM booster, McDonnell Aircraft Corporation was to provide the Gemini B capsule, General Electric Company was to provide the mission module equipment and experiment integration, Eastman Kodak was to provide the photographic equipment, and Hamilton Standard was to provide the pressure suit. The largest contract was signed with Douglas Aircraft Company to develop the laboratory vehicle and mission module structure, and to provide the systems integration.[103] A number of subcontractors were also involved with developing everything from the communications system (Collins radio) to the laboratory's waste management system (Fairchild-Hiller).[104]

James Ferguson. Source: USAF.

Gerald F. Keeling. Source: USAF.

An Updated Management Approach

The MOL Program Office continued to evolve as program needs changed. In September 1966, General Schriever retired, and the Secretary of the Air Force named General James Ferguson as Director of MOL.[105] In February 1967, General Ferguson established the MOL Executive Council to provide a forum for discussion of major problem areas and exchange of views.[106] Council members included the Director of MOL, the Vice Director of MOL, the Deputy Director of MOL, the Commander Space Systems Division, the Director of Special Projects, and representatives from each of the major MOL contractors.[107] In June 1967, Secretary of the Air Force Harold Brown named Major General Gerald F. Keeling, in addition to his duties as Deputy Chief of Staff, Procurement and Production at Air Force Headquarters, as Assistant Director of MOL for Procurement.[108] MOL was moving into a new phase of program development.

In May 1967, contractors and MOL officials signed definitive contracts, initiating the engineering development phase of the program or Phase II.[109] The preceding month, Brig. Gen. Martin voiced his concerns to DNRO Flax that the current management structure, divided by "black" and "white" contracts, was no longer effective as the program entered Phase II. Brig. Gen. Martin argued that the reconnaissance payload, arguably the only reason the MOL program existed, had evolved into something far more complex and involved interfaces throughout the MOL system. Brig. Gen. Martin urged the DNRO to give executive responsibility of both black and white contracts to him, the Director of SAFSP.[110] In June, the Air Force MOL Policy Committee weighed in, "It has become increasingly apparent that present assignments of program responsibilities to SAFSP and the MOL Systems Office are not conducive to the best possible Government management of this complex and costly system… It is now proposed to assign essentially all base-line program responsibility to the MOL Systems Office."[111] It was clear that changes were necessary.

In order to address the concerns of those involved and accommodate the new phase of the program, under General Ferguson's direction, MOL adopted an updated management approach on 1 July 1967.[112] Under the new agreement, the Secretary of the Air Force and DNRO were jointly in charge of the executive management of MOL. The Secretary of the Air Force was responsible for all Air Force decisions pertaining to MOL, while the DNRO was to advise on all interfaces with the National Reconnaissance Program and was responsible for all NRP aspects of MOL.[113] Together, the Secretary of the Air Force and the DNRO would assign responsibility and delegate authority to the Director of MOL. The Director of MOL was now responsible to both the Secretary of the Air Force and the DNRO for development, acquisition, and testing of the total MOL system in the approved baseline program, including the Dorian payload.[114] With these new changes, "the Director, MOL has greater responsibility and broader authority than is usual in an Air Force development program."[115]

This streamlined management approach necessitated access to information and collective judgment through additional channels. In response, four committees were formed: the MOL Policy Committee advised the Secretary of the Air Force on program objectives, management and fiscal matters, and interdepartmental and interagency matters; the Program Review Council assisted the Secretary of the Air Force and DNRO in discharge of their executive management responsibilities for MOL; the Internal Management Group assisted the Director of MOL in his management function; and the MOL Executive Council was a forum for discussions among top-level government and contractor management of major problem areas and for the exchange of views and information on overall program matters.[116] Contrary to what Brig. Gen. Martin had requested, the Director of SAFSP now provided reconnaissance satellite experience to MOL through membership on the MOL Program Review Council.[117] He continued to play a role in certain sensor technology contracts, which would be executed later in the program, as well as implementing security within the MOL Program.[118] But in general, Brig. Gen. Martin's responsibilities were far more limited than he had proposed.

> *"Let's build this damn thing and make it work."*

In accordance with this change, recently promoted Major General Joseph Bleymaier replaced Brig. Gen. Berg as Deputy Director, MOL.[119] Maj. Gen. Bleymaier had been involved with the program from the very beginning and proved to be an effective manager for the bulk of the life of the program. Captain Robert Crippen recalled, "General Bleymaier was the guy that was the big boss at that time. We interfaced with him."[120] Colonel Lachlan Macleay stated, "Bleymaier was involved in the day-to-day, 'Let's build this damn thing and make it work.'"[121] Macleay recollected that Bleymaier was an effective leader, "General Bleymaier was a great manager. I wasn't in his every day meetings, but when you were around him, he had a way of looking at things that made sense."[122] Macleay fondly remembered other program leadership as well. He recollected, "There were other good people, very capable. Larry Skantze ended up being head of the Systems Command, 4-star general. He was on the program... Buck Buchanan who was kind of our boss was another very capable guy."[123]

Through persistence and determination, leadership had fought to gain the necessary approvals for MOL, a groundbreaking program. With approvals and capable leadership in place, MOL management turned their attention to identifying individuals who were both technically savvy and adventurous to man the program. The program was experimental. As such, MOL required individuals to design and operate it who were creative and comfortable pushing boundaries and exploring the unknown. Through a rigorous selection process, seventeen individuals were eventually selected to serve as MOL crew members. MOL had certainly found and retained talented management – they also eventually found talented crew.

Endnotes

1. T.A. Heppenheimer, *The Space Shuttle Decision, 1965-1972: History of the Space Shuttle Volume 1* (Washington, D.C.: Smithsonian Institution Scholarly Press, 2002), p. 50-54; Vance O. Mitchell, *Sharing Space* (Virginia: The National Reconnaissance Office, 2012), p. 42.

2. Memorandum for Director, MOL, Eugene Zuckert, Sub: Authorization to Proceed with MOL Program, 25 August 1962, Job 199700050-02-003-014, NROARC.

3. News Release, Sub: AF to Develop MOL, 10 December 1963, Job 199700050-02-002-019, NROARC.

4. Joint Message from OSAF (General John L. Martin) to ALMAJCOM, 10 December 1963, Job 199700076-02-004-009, NROARC.

5. Carl Berger, *History of the Manned Orbiting Laboratory Program (MOL)*, (Washington, D.C.: MOL Program Office, Department of the Air Force, 1970), p. 60.

6. Memorandum, Brockway McMillan (Undersecretary of the AF) to Deputy Chief of Staff R&D, Sub: Requirements and Objectives for the MOL Program, 15 January 1964, Job 199700050-02-002-024, NROARC.

7. Vance Mitchell, *Sharing Space, (Chantilly, Virginia: the National Reconnaissance Office, 2012), p. 42-44*.

8. Preliminary Technical Development Plan for MOL, April 1964, Job 199900021-07-009, NROARC.

9. Memorandum, Harold Brown to Secretary of Defense, Sub: Initiation of MOL Pre-Phase I, 21 April 1964, Job 199700050-02-002-033, NROARC.

10. Letter, McMillan to Schriever, 6 April 1964, Job 199700070-03-007-008, NROARC.

11. Memorandum, Harold Brown to Secretary of Defense, Sub: Initiation of MOL Pre-Phase I, 21 April 1964, Job 199700050-02-002-033, NROARC.

12. Memorandum, William Brady, System Program Director for MOL to SSG-1, Sub: Gemini/MOL Experiments, 2 December 1964, Job 199900089-03-019-001, NROARC.

13. Memorandum, to Bleymaier, Sub: Qualified Contracts to Receive MOL RFP, January 1965, Job 199700043-03-001-004, NROARC.

14. Memorandum, Zuckert to Chief of Staff, USAF, Sub: Authorization to Award Contracts for MOL Preliminary Design Studies, 26 February 1965, Job 199700043-03-001-009, NROARC.

15. Memorandum, Brigadier General Harry Evans to General Blanchard, Sub: MOL Contractor Information, July 1965, Job 199700057-02-001-015, NROARC.

16. Manned Orbital Laboratory Technical Panel First Preliminary Report, Job 199900021-01-024-044, NROARC.

17. Memorandum for Record, signed McMillan, Sub: Reconnaissance Experiments in MOL, 26 March 1964, Job 199700070-03-007-008, NROARC.

18. Notes on Draft Memorandum, Sub: MOL Experiments, dated after 3 February 1964, Job 199700033-09-018-022, NROARC.

19. Ibid.

20. Memorandum, Albert C. Hall (Deputy Director for Space) and Bruno W Augenstein (Special Assistance, Intelligence and Reconnaissance) to Dr. Brown and Dr. Fubini, Sub: Experiments for the MOL, and the purpose of the MOL Program, 5 March 1964, Job 199700050-02-002-030, NROARC.

21. Ibid.

22. Memorandum, McMillan to Colonel Schultz (Assistant for MOL, AFRMO), 2 July 1964, Job 199700050-02-002-038, NROARC.

23. Primary Experiments Data for the MOL Program, March 1965, Job 199900021-07-012, NROARC.

24. Memorandum, Flax to Deputy Chief of Staff, Research and Development, Sub: MOL Schedule Alternatives, 3 August 1964, Job 199700050-02-002-040, NROARC.

25 Letter, Schriever to General JP McConnell (Chief of Staff, USAF), 12 June 1965, Job 199700043-03-001-012, NROARC.

26 Ibid.

27 Memorandum, Brown to Undersecretary of the Air Force, Sub: MOL, 4 January 1965, Job 199700083-13-002F, NROARC.

28 Ibid.

29 Ibid.

30 "The Need for Very High Resolution Imagery and its Contribution to DOD Operations and Decisions. Volume I – Executive Summary," November 1968, Job 199700057-05-001, NROARC.

31 Briefing notes, LtCol Byron F. Knolle, Jr (Deputy Director SP-11) to DDR&E, 16 January 1965, Job 199900019-10-005, NROARC.

32 Ibid.

33 Memorandum, Hornig to Secretary of Defense, 30 June 1965, Job 199700050-02-003-010, NROARC.

34 Ibid.

35 Ibid.

36 Memorandum, Hornig to President Johnson, 30 June 1965, Job 199700050-02-003-010, NROARC.

37 Berger, *History of the Manned Orbiting Laboratory Program*, p. 121.

38 Memorandum, Mazza to Evans and Stewart, Sub: DOD/MOL Program Security, 18 May 1965, Job 199700070-03-007-020, NROARC.

39 Ibid.

40 Ibid.

41 Letter, Jeffrey C. Kitchen (Deputy Assist Secretary for Politico-Military Affairs) to John T. McNaughton (Assistant Secretary for International Security Affairs, Department of Defense), 25 March 1964, Job 199700033-09-018-020, NROARC.

42 Memorandum, Spurgeon M Keeny, Jr (Initialed by McGeorge Bundy) to Vice President Humphrey, Sub: Organization and Public Position on MOL, 8 July 1965, Job 200800072-09-009-007, NROARC.

43 Memorandum for Record, Colonel Paul Worthman, Sub: MOL "Posture" Paper, 13 July 1965, Job 199700057-04-010-022, NROARC.

44 Ibid.

45 Policy on Public Information Aspects and International Reactions to the Manned Orbiting Laboratory, 26 July 1965, Job 199700083-13-002C, NROARC.

46 Colonel Paul Worthman, Policy on Public Information Aspects and International Reactions to the MOL, 26 July 1965, Job 199700057-04-010-018, NROARC.

47 Memorandum, W.F. Raborn to McNamara, Sub: MOL, 21 July 1965, Job 199700046-05-009, NROARC.

48 Memorandum for Record, Col Worthman, Sub: USIB Endorsement of MOL Photographic Capability, 27 July 1965, Job 199700057-04-010-015, NROARC.

49 Memorandum, McNamara to President, Sub: MOL, undated, Job 199700057-04-010-011, NROARC.

50 Ibid.

51 Oral Interview with Larry Glass, 1 April 2014, p. 3, CSNR/RC.

52 Memorandum, McNamara to President Johnson, Sub: MOL, undated, Job 199700057-04-010-011, NROARC.

53 Memorandum for Record, Col Worthman, Sub: Proposed MOL Press Release, 27 July 1965, Job 199700057-04-010-014, NROARC.

54   Memorandum, McNamara to President Johnson, Sub: MOL, undated, Job 199700057-04-010-011, NROARC.

55   Letter, McMillan to Schriever, Sub: MOL management, 6 February 1964, Job 199700050-02-002-028, NROARC.

56   Memorandum, Evans to McMillan and Schriever, Sub: MOL Management, 5 July 1965, Job 199700070-03-009-008, NROARC.

57   Management of the MOL Program No. 65-1, 25 August 1965, Job 199700050-02-004-003, NROARC.

58   Secretary of the Air Force Order, signed by Eugene Zuckert (Secretary of the Air Force), Sub: Director of the MOL Program, 25 August 1965, Job 199700050-02-004-005, NROARC.

59   Memorandum for Record, Col Worthman, Sub: Proposed MOL Press Release, 27 July 1965, Job 199700057-04-010-014, NROARC. Memorandum for Record, Col Worthman, Sub: MOL Policy Questions, 27 July 1965, 199700057-04-010-017, NROARC.

60   Memorandum for Record, Col Worthman, Sub: MOL Policy Questions, 27 July 1965, Job 199700057-04-010-017, NROARC.

61   President Johnson's Statement on MOL – Press Conference, 25 August 1965, Job 199700033-09-018-008, NROARC.

62   Memorandum, to the Secretary of Defense, Sub: MOL Management, undated, Job 199700076-02-004-018, NROARC.

63   Berger, *History of the Manned Orbiting Laboratory*, p. 143.

64   Message, Major Robert Herman (SAF-OIPC), 30 August 1965, Job 199700083-13-002A, NROARC.

65   Government Plan for Program Management for the Manned Orbiting Laboratory System (MOL) Program, 1 September 1966, NROARC.

66   Ibid.

67   Procedural Considerations for MOL Program Management, signed by DNRO Flax and Director, MOL Schriever, undated, Job 199700070-03-008-012, NROARC.

68   Memorandum, signed by Martin and Schriever, Sub: Agreement Concerning MOL System Program Office and Program Management, September 1965, Job 199900021-01-024-036, NROARC.

69   Memorandum, Schriever to Secretary of the Air Force, Sub: MOL Monthly Status Report for November 1965, 9 December 1965, Job 199700033-08-024-001, NROARC.

70   Procedural Considerations for MOL Program Management, signed by DNRO Flax and Director, MOL Schriever, undated, Job 199700070-03-008-012, NROARC.

71   Berger, *History of the Manned Orbiting Laboratory Program*, p. 147.

72   Berger, *History of the Manned Orbiting Laboratory Program*, p. 145.

73   Memorandum, Col Worthman to Stewart, Sub: Your Relationship to the DORIAN Program, 28 September 1965, Job 199700070-03-008-006, NROARC.

74   MOL Program Background, 8 June 1969, Job 199700066-05-005-002, NROARC.

75   Manned Orbiting Laboratory Program Plan volume 2 of 2, 15 June 1967, Job 199700066-05-015, NROARC.

76   Manned Orbiting Laboratory Program Plan Volume 1 of 2, undated, Job 199700066-05-014, NROARC.

77   Memorandum, to Deputy Director, MOL, Sub: Designation of MOL as the KH-10 Photographic Reconnaissance Satellite System, 14 February 1969, Job 199700073-05-003-006, NROARC.

78   Manned Orbiting Laboratory Program Plan volume 2 of 2, 15 June 1967, Job 199700066-05-015, NROARC.

79   MOL Program Background, 8 June 1969, Job 199700066-05-005-002, NROARC.

80   Ibid.

81   Manned Orbiting Laboratory Program Plan volume 2 of 2, 15 June 1967, Job 199700066-05-015, NROARC.

82   Ibid.

83   Oral Interview with Robert Crippen, 24 March 2014, p. 13, CSNR/RC.

84   Manned Orbiting Laboratory Program Plan Volume 1 of 2, undated, Job 199700066-05-014, NROARC.

85   Memorandum, Flax to Assistant Secretary of the Army, Research and Development, Sub: MOL, 6 April 1966, Job 199700050-02-005-009, NROARC.

86   Oral interview with Richard Truly, 4 June 2014, p. 6, CSNR/RC.

87   Preliminary Performance/Design Requirements for MOL System, January 1966, Job 199900019-14-024, NROARC.

88   Oral interview with Lachlan Macleay, 2 June 2014, p. 9, CSNR/RC.

89   MOL Program Background, 8 June 1969, Job 199700066-05-005-002, NROARC.

90   Memorandum, Department of State to American embassy SANTIAGO, 22 October 1966, Job 199700050-02-008-004, NROARC.

91   Memorandum, signed by James Stewart for James Ferguson to Secretary of the Air Force, Sub: MOL Monthly Status Report for July, 6 August 1968, Job 199700033-08-029E, NROARC.

92   Manned Orbiting Laboratory Program Plan Volume 1 of 2, undated, Job 199700066-05-014, NROARC.

93   Agenda and highlights: Air Force MOL Policy Committee Meeting, 14 October 1965, Job 199700097-08-030-3, NROARC.

94   Manned Orbiting Laboratory Program Plan Volume 1 of 2, undated, Job 199700066-05-014, NROARC.

95   Manned Orbiting Laboratory Program Plan volume 2 of 2, 15 June 1967, Job 199700066-05-015, NROARC.

96   Preliminary Performance/Design Requirements for MOL System, January 1966, Job 199900019-14-024, NROARC.

97   Ibid.

98   Oral Interview with Richard Truly, 4 June 2014, p. 6, CSNR/RC.

99   Agenda and highlights: Air Force MOL Policy Committee Meeting, 14 October 1965, Job 199700097-08-030-3, NROARC.

100 Letter, Evans to Russell Berg, 4 January 1966, Job 199700076-02-005-015, NROARC.

101 Ibid.

102 Memorandum, Major General E.B. LeBailly, Sub: Manned Orbiting Laboratory (MOL) Information Plan, 10 January 1966, Job 199700057-01-002-021, NROARC.

103 Memorandum, Sub: MOL Program, 24 July 1967, Job 199900021-03-005, NROARC.

104 Briefing Charts, Sub: Executive Session – MOL Program Review, 14 June 1967, Job 199700066-05-011, NROARC.

105 Secretary of the Air Force Order, Harold Brown, Sub: Director of MOL Program, 1 September 1966, Job 199700050-02-007-005, NROARC.

106 MOL Program Office Instruction No. 2: MOL Executive Council Management Meetings, signed by James Ferguson, 25 February 1967, Job 199700033-08-001-008, NROARC.

107 Ibid.

108 Memorandum, Brown to Major General G. F. Keeling, Sub: Delegation of Special Authority to the Head of a Procuring Activity, 20 June 1967, Job 199900021-01-024-009, NROARC.

109 Memorandum, Sub: MOL Program, 24 July 1967, Job 199900021-03-005, NROARC.

110 Memorandum, Sub: Management issues, April 1967, Job 199700070-03-009-016, NROARC.

111 Memorandum, Sub: Air Force MOL Policy Committee Highlight Summary of Agenda Items for meeting 67-1, 1 June 1967, Job 199700033-09-016-017, NROARC.

112 Manned Orbiting Laboratory Program Plan Volume 1 of 2, undated, Job 199700066-05-014, NROARC.

113 Ibid.

114 Memorandum, Stewart to Secretary of the Air Force, Sub: MOL Monthly Status Report for May, 5 June 1967, Job 199700033-08-027H, NROARC.

115 MOL Program Office Instruction No. 3, Sub: MOL Program Management Activities, Ferguson, 1 December 1967, Job 199700070-03-009-023, NROARC.

116 Ibid.

117 Manned Orbiting Laboratory Program Plan Volume 1 of 2, undated, Job 199700066-05-014, NROARC.

118 Ibid.

119 Memorandum, Stewart and Ferguson to Secretary of the Air Force, Sub: MOL Monthly Status Report for July, 7 August 1967, Job 199700033-08-028B, NROARC.

120 Oral Interview with Robert Crippen, 24 March 2014, p. 7, CSNR/RC.

121 Oral Interview with Lachlan Macleay, 2 June 2014, p. 16, CSNR/RC.

122 Ibid, p. 19.

123 Ibid, p. 19.

Chapter 2

THE MOL PILOTS

By 1965, with a vision of what man in space could accomplish for national defense and security, MOL leadership was prepared to staff the program. The process was highly selective, and ultimately seventeen talented individuals were selected from across the services to push boundaries and explore man's contributions.

Selecting the First Group

Due to strict security requirements and a need to select the best of the best, the selection process for MOL was long and involved, and none of the candidates knew very much about the program. Lachlan Macleay recalled, "I didn't volunteer to get on the list. In other words, there was, to my knowledge, no open application process to get on MOL."[1] Richard Truly recalled a similar experience, "As the year went on, in the fall of that year, the students realized that something was going on. What I understand is that Yeager [commandant of the school] had convinced the Air Force that when they selected the first set of crew to the MOL program, they should all be graduates of the Aerospace Research Pilot School (ARPS). Counting our class, there were only 85 graduates at that time. The second assumption that Yeager made was that all of them wanted to do it. So I never filled out an application, I never applied. They ran the selection of those 85 people without telling us. They finally narrowed it to I think 15 finalists, and my name was in it, and so was Jack Finley who was a classmate of mine and another Navy lieutenant."[2] Truly later teased, "I was in a program, and I never applied."[3]

In addition to choosing smart, talented pilots, there were physical considerations as well. Macleay explained, "I had tried for NASA several times and been rejected because I was too tall. They had a 6-foot height limit and that was it. They didn't care who you were, you could have been Einstein; if you were 6-foot-1, they wouldn't take you."[4] Given those restrictions, prior to the series of physicals the entire group had to endure, Macleay and two other candidates were sent to Houston. Macleay recalled of the experience, "They sent us down to Houston to put us in a full pressure suit to see whether or not we would fit in the Gemini capsule… The only full pressure suit they had that was for somebody halfway sized was Walt Schirra. Well he was only 5'11". I got in his suit, and it hurt. I got in there and I took the chin strap and I pulled it down so damn hard, I was bound and determined I was going to make it. I pulled it so hard it almost hurt. I can remember… the guy that was down there to see whether we would fit, he took his hand and he rubbed it between my head and the top and he said, 'Yeah, he'll fit.' And that was it."[5]

The physicals were grueling as well. Macleay recollected, "The next thing we did was we took a hell of a physical. They sent us down to Brooks Aero Med Lab in San Antonio. They gave us an eight-day physical. It was something else. They poked and prodded and all kinds of things, everything from psychiatric to frustration machines to blood pressure. They had a sugar tolerance test where you got stabbed in the arm every 30 minutes for 4 hours or something. They had every test you could think of."[6] One test in particular that Macleay remembers well was a carotid artery test. "They had a test where they had you all wired-up. They did this whole carotid artery thing, cut off your carotid artery and see what happened to your brain. Well with me, they pressed like hell on one side, and they didn't get anything. They pressed on the other side, and in about one second I was out."[7] Initially disqualified for failing the test, Macleay was able to pass other tests and use his experience to remain on the list. Meanwhile, the number of qualified candidates continued to drop.

After background investigations and psychological, physical, and psychiatric examinations, the final step in the qualification process was the interview. With the group narrowed down to about 12 or 13 candidates, Macleay remembered, "We all sat out in the hall and got called in one at a time. The board consisted of Chuck Yeager, who was the commandant of the test pilot school at the time, a famous test pilot; the surgeon general of the Systems' Command, and I forget his name now; and some other people I didn't know, but all pretty high-ranking officers. You went through an interview. 'Why do you want to do this? What's your background?'"[8] The interviews had some light moments, too. Most of the pilots were Air Force, while Truly and Finley were from the Navy. Macleay recalled, "Yeager asked Dick, 'Why decide to fly in the Navy?' And Dick said something about, 'Well two-thirds of the earth's surface is covered with water.' And Yeager said, 'One-hundred percent is covered with air.'"[9] Following the interviews, the final eight were selected. According to MOL policy, the final decision ultimately rested with the MOL Director, General Bernard A. Schriever.[10]

Through all the tests and physicals and interviews, no one knew exactly what they were getting into. Albert Crews, selected in the first cadre, claimed, "It was a very classified program. We weren't briefed on the program until after we were selected. Then we were told that we could leave if we didn't like what we were doing."[11] Without security clearances prior to selection, Crews explained, "I never knew anything about reconnaissance until we were selected because they couldn't talk about it unless you had the proper clearance, and none of us had that clearance until after we were selected… We had been selected and then at least a month into the program before we were ever briefed on the reconnaissance mission."[12] Macleay also recalled, "Now when we were going through the MOL selection process, nobody knew what the hell it was. I mean it was just going to be some flying laboratory, and that was the story. But I don't think anybody really thought they were going to sit and watch the life of fleas or something in space. I thought there would be some military application."[13] Although Truly had been kept at Edwards an extra year to maintain eligibility for the program, even he did not know what the program was about. He explained, "Of course MOL had this enormous cover story, I would call it, which was the public MOL program to learn about how man could operate in space and do experiments that would be advantageous to the military. That's all I knew about the program, and any of us knew, until the day after the press conference when we were announced."[14]

The layers of secrecy started to fall away after they were announced and their clearances came through. James Abrahamson, selected in the third group, explained, "The first part of it was to get introduced to what real classification was and, secondly, what the satellite surveillance program was, then what MOL was going to be about."[15] Truly recalled of the experience, "It was one of the most amazing days of my entire career because we got briefed on all these code words - Dorian and Gambit and Hexagon, TK, all these different code words. Every view graph was covered with them. And of course at that time, the NRO was covert, none of these organizations existed. None of the programs existed in the public eye. And yet they were doing great things. It gave me great confidence in the United States that they could pull off such an enormous technological effort and still be invisible. It didn't exist. It was amazing… It was an introduction not to one but to two space programs: the public, what the public knew and astronauts and all that jazz, and then this other world of capability that didn't exist."[16] Truly stated further, "When I was introduced to the program, it was stunning. It was almost magic… I marveled that the government could pull off what was right before my very eyes."[17]

The First Group of MOL Pilots

The first group of eight MOL crew members was selected in the fall of 1965. They received their initial briefing into the program at Space Systems Division on 16 October by Brig. Gen. Berg and were expected on station in early December.[18] On 12 November at the Air Force Systems Command's Space System division headquarters at the Los Angeles Air Force Station, the Air Force held a press conference to introduce all eight: Michael J. Adams, Albert H. Crews, Jr., John L. Finley, Richard E. Lawyer, Lachlan Macleay, Francis G. Neubeck, James M. Taylor, and Richard H. Truly.[19] Given the security constraints of the program, the Air Force hoped to answer basic questions, but also keep public information minimal and low-impact. As Macleay recalled, "They were going to announce it on a Friday afternoon so it would miss the news. It would be in the dead news day, and we wouldn't get a lot of attention."[20] At the press conference, the Air Force distributed pictures and short biographies of the eight crew members, a short MOL factsheet, and copies of the statement President Johnson issued on 25 August approving the program.[21] Due to the classified nature of the program, however, as Truly later explained, "That press conference was going to be the first and last because the Air Force and the NRO didn't want us going near the press."[22] Optimistic about the future of the program, the Air Force also announced that 12 more crew members would soon be chosen.

Michael J. Adams.
Source: CSNR Reference Collection.

At 35 years old, Michael James Adams joined the MOL program with an impressive career already behind him. He was born in Sacramento, California on 5 May 1930 and graduated from Sacramento Junior College before enlisting in the Air Force in 1950. Adams earned his pilot wings at Webb Air Force Base in Texas in 1952, then served as a fighter-bomber pilot during the Korean War. After being stationed in Louisiana and France, Adams returned to school at the University of Oklahoma; he received his aeronautical engineering degree there in 1958. Next, Adams studied astronautics at the Massachusetts Institute of Technology (MIT) for about 18 months before he was selected for the Experimental Test Pilot School at Edwards Air Force Base in California in 1962. While at Edwards, Adams was awarded the Honts Trophy for best scholar and pilot in his class. Adams then attended the Aerospace Research Pilot School, where he was one of only four pilots to participate in a five-month series of NASA moon landing practice tests at the Martin Company in Baltimore, Maryland. Adams graduated with honors in December 1963. While Adams was in the first group of MOL pilots selected, he

MOL group 1 astronauts. From left to right: Adams, Crews, Finley, Lawyer, Macleay, Neubeck, Taylor, Truly.
Source: CSNR Reference Collection.

was also the first to leave. He was selected for the X-15 program, a joint Air Force/NASA project, in July 1966. After a number of successful flights, tragedy struck on 15 November 1967, and Adams was killed in an X-15 accident. Adams reached an altitude of over 50 statute miles on his final flight and was posthumously awarded his Astronaut Wings.[23] It was a devastating loss for all who knew him.

Albert Hanlin Crews, Jr. was the oldest of the first group selected. He was born on 23 March 1929 in El Dorado, Arkansas. Crews studied chemical engineering at the University of Southwestern Louisiana, graduating with his Bachelor of Science degree in 1950. After graduation, Crews claimed, "I joined the Air Force in 1950 to avoid the draft. I applied for Aviation Cadets. I learned to fly and was in a fighter squadron for about five years"[24] in Tripoli, Libya. Next, Crews recalled, "I decided the same people that were flight commanders and my bosses were the same people that were there when I started, so I applied to go back to school. I was allowed to go to the [Air Force] Institute of Technology (AFIT). They told me I could get a master's degree in aeronautical engineering,"[25] which Crews did pursue. He recalled, "I was attending AFIT, about half-way through, when Sputnik flew. Then when they picked the seven astronauts, that impressed me... I decided then that I wanted to be an astronaut."[26] While finishing school, Crews applied for and was accepted to the Test Pilot School at Edwards, graduating in 1960. After about three years at Edwards, in September 1962, Crews was selected with five others to participate in the DynaSoar or X-20 program, replacing Neil Armstrong who transferred to NASA Houston. When DynaSoar was canceled, Crews spent some time working on experiments which eventually flew on Skylab, although he was ultimately transferred to MOL.

Albert H. Crews.
Source: CSNR Reference Collection.

MOL group 1 astronauts. From left to right: Crews, Truly, Lawyer, Taylor, Neubeck, Adams, Macleay, Finley.
Source: CSNR Reference Collection.

John L. Finley.
Source: CSNR Reference Collection.

Richard E. Lawyer.
Source: CSNR Reference Collection.

Lachlan Macleay.
Source: CSNR Reference Collection.

John Lawrence Finley was one of two members of the Navy selected for the first MOL cadre. He was born on 22 December 1935 in Winchester, Massachusetts and graduated from the U.S. Naval Academy at Annapolis in 1957. After Finley completed flight training in Florida in August 1958, he spent four years flying F-8 aircraft aboard the USS *Ticonderoga*. Finley was briefly assigned as the senior landing signal officer (LSO) of Carrier Air Wing Five before he transferred to the ARPS at Edwards in 1964. Finley was working as an instructor at ARPS when he was selected to join the MOL program in 1965 – a deliberate assignment to prevent the MOL program from losing him back to the Navy. Frustrated with the number of delays in the program, Finley requested a transfer back to the operational Navy in April 1968.[27]

Known for his passion for the outdoors, his dry sense of humor, and his unending humility, Richard "Dick" Earl Lawyer was born in Los Angeles on 8 November 1932. Following his graduation from the University of California at Berkeley with a degree in aeronautical engineering in 1955, Lawyer began his Air Force pilot training. In the ten years between college graduation and being selected for the MOL program, Lawyer finished as a distinguished graduate from the Air Force Fighter Weapons School and served two combat tours during the Vietnam War. In 1958, Lawyer was part of a squadron chosen to test the F-105B aircraft, launching his career as a flight test pilot. Lawyer then attended the Air Force's ARPS at Edwards Air Force Base, earning the Honts award as outstanding member of his class for academic achievement and flying excellence. He was an instructor at ARPS when he was selected for the MOL program.[28]

Lachlan "Mac" Macleay was born in St. Louis, Missouri on 13 June 1931. Although he graduated from the Naval Academy in Annapolis with a Bachelor of Science degree in electrical engineering in 1954, Macleay explained, "I took a commission in the Air Force along with about 25% of my classmates."[29] After completing flight training, Macleay became an F-86 instructor at both Tyndall and Moody Air Force Bases. Next, Macleay recalled, "[I] applied for and was accepted to the test pilot school in the class of '58. I graduated in August of '60 and was assigned to Special Projects at Edwards Air Force Base which basically was flying U-2s, basically as a test bed for a lot of things."[30] Macleay was assigned to a remote tour in Korea to help get the 109th fighter wing combat ready, before returning home just in time for the Cuban Missile Crisis. At that point, he was "deployed again in the U-2 stand at Patrick Air Force Base, Florida."[31] Next, Macleay recollected, "I applied for and was accepted at the Aerospace Research Pilot School, which was the follow-on course for potential astronaut trainees."[32] While there, Macleay participated in a variety of training opportunities that prepared him for what was to come in MOL. He explained, "We had classroom work, orbital mechanics, thermodynamics, pretty technical stuff. The flying part was

Francis G. Neubeck.
Source: CSNR Reference Collection.

James M. Taylor.
Source: CSNR Reference Collection.

Richard H. Truly.
Source: CSNR Reference Collection.

very interesting."[33] While there, one of Macleay's instructors was Hank Hartsfield who was chosen the following year to join the MOL program. After graduation, Macleay remained at Edwards and served as a project pilot for the F-4C and F-5 aircraft. From Edwards, Macleay was eventually selected for the MOL program.

Like Lachlan Macleay, Francis Gregory Neubeck graduated from the Naval Academy, a year after Macleay in 1955, and elected to join the Air Force. Neubeck was born in Washington, D.C. on 11 April 1932. After Annapolis, his first assignment was at Eglin Air Force Base as a flight instructor, and he later began developing weapons systems for jet fighters. Neubeck attended both the Air Force's Test Pilot School at Edwards in 1960 and the Aerospace Research Pilot School in 1962. Neubeck was still stationed at Eglin when he was selected for the MOL program.[34]

James Martin Taylor was born on 27 November 1930 in Stamps, Arkansas. He received his associate's degree from Southern State University in 1950 before enlisting in the Air Force the following year. He became an aviation cadet in 1952 and earned his pilot's wings in 1953. Taylor returned to school and earned his bachelor's degree in electrical engineering in 1959 from the University of Michigan, after which he served as a flight test engineer for bombers and cargo aircraft. In 1963, Taylor graduated from the Air Force Test Pilot School at Edwards. He then completed the Aerospace Research Pilot School before he was selected for MOL.[35]

The youngest crew member of the original eight, Richard "Dick" Harrison Truly was born in Fayette, Mississippi on 12 November 1937. Recalling his early years, he stated, "I went to college at Georgia Tech on a Naval ROTC scholarship. I got a degree in aeronautical engineering [in 1959]. When I graduated, I applied to go to flight training; the Navy sent me to Beeville in Texas to train."[36] Truly was designated a Naval Aviator on 7 October 1960 and recalled, "The Navy ordered me to fighter squadron 33 which was aboard the *Intrepid* and later *Enterprise*. I flew carrier operations in that squadron, flying the F-8 Crusader."[37] In 1963, he was selected to attend ARPS at Edwards Air Force Base. Truly reminisced, "It was a year-long course. The first six months were test pilot training, and the second six months were space-related training because at that time, of course this was 1964, NASA was building up Mercury, Gemini, and later Apollo."[38] By this point, the initial MOL selection process was underway and, as Truly recalled, "The Air Force was afraid, and they were probably right, that if the Navy had given me a set of orders back to the fleet, the chances were they'd never have seen me again. So Yeager... advised the Navy that Finley and I had been identified for the first crew, but the crew hadn't been publicly announced. So to keep their hands on us, we were kept at Edwards the next year as instructors in the Test Pilot School."[39]

Selecting the Second Group

The MOL program was revealed to the public during the Air Force press conference in November 1965, and the first group of MOL pilots was chosen before selection began for the second group. Given these new circumstances, the selection process for the second group differed from the first in one important way – the candidates had a slightly better idea of what they were pursuing. As Robert Crippen, a member of the second group, recalled, "While I was at [the Test Pilot] school, the notices were sent out by, as I said, both NASA and the DoD to everybody in the school because everybody wanted to go apply for it. It was pretty common knowledge at the school at the time."[40] With strict restrictions in place, however, applicants' knowledge of the program was limited. Crippen knew a number of the original group selected, but that was about all he knew. He recalled, "Since it was very highly classified, all I knew was the program existed, they were planning on flying out of Vandenberg Air Force Base, and it was highly classified."[41] This was not unusual for the field, however. Crippen described the entire field of space reconnaissance, "It didn't exist. It was all highly classified and compartmentalized programs. You had a 'need to know.' It was the kind of thing where you had to get a personal introduction to anybody to even talk about the program."[42]

Karol Bobko, a MOL pilot selected in the second group, recalled applying to be an astronaut, although the divisions between NASA and the DoD were hazy. He stated, "I don't know how they selected who was going to NASA or who was going into the Air Force, or to the MOL program. They just said, 'You people have been selected as part of the MOL program, or as the finalists in the MOL program, while the others were the finalists in NASA.' But it wasn't clear to me, anyhow, how that all occurred."[43] The process itself mirrored that which the first group of pilots endured with applications, physicals, and interviews.

The public announcement of the second group of pilots was similar to that of the first. On 17 June 1966, at Space Systems Division headquarters in California, with no national news coverage, the announcement was made in front of ten newsmen. As described in a memorandum from recently promoted Major General Evans to General Schriever, "It appears that the objective of a low key introduction was accomplished with the story receiving only hometown news treatment."[44]

Even after they were announced, the second group still had to wait on security before they could be fully introduced to the program. Crippen remembered, "After we were selected, it was supposedly giving us more education, but we stayed on at the school and studied some more advanced subjects while they ran through our security compliance. So we really didn't have, initially, too much contact with the program itself. But after that was cleared, we reported in to what was at that time SAMSO or Space and Missile Systems Organization in Los Angeles International."[45] Once they did report and began working on the program, they were quickly welcomed by the first group – many of whom they knew through the Test Pilot School. Bobko recalled, "These aren't big groups of people. Some of the people we had already known through the Test Pilot School or through testing in the area, so it was a rather small group."[46] He further explained, "The group wasn't so big, so we all worked together. The first seven certainly were the first seven [Michael J. Adams had already left the program at this point, bringing the first group down to seven pilots]. But I thought that they welcomed us rather well."[47] Although some divisions did remain, Albert Crews recalled welcoming the second group into the program, "We, as much as we could, tried to be a total group for what was going on… I don't remember any problems, but we were of the opinion that the first flights would come out of the first group."[48]

In The Words of Those Who Served

The Second Group of MOL Pilots

Around the time the first group of pilots was announced, the Air Force began the selection process for the second group. During November 1965, the Personnel Center at Randolph Air Force Base began screening over 500 applications for astronaut duty with either NASA or MOL.[49] The selection board forwarded 100 nominees to Air Force Headquarters, in general order of merit. From there, the MOL Chief of Staff nominated 25 applicants to the Director of MOL for further selection.[50] During April 1966, the MOL Program Office screened all 25 candidates and recommended to the MOL Director that five selectees – three Air Force, one Navy, and one Marine Corps officer – be assigned to MOL.[51] Some of the finalists who were not selected were scheduled to instead attend the Air Force's Aerospace Research Pilot School at Edwards and be reconsidered for the planned third group of pilots.[52] The next round of MOL test pilots – Karol J. Bobko, Robert L. Crippen, C. Gordon Fullerton, Henry W. Hartsfield, and Robert F. Overmyer – were approved and publicly announced on 17 June 1966.

MOL group 2 astronauts. From left to right: Overmyer, Hartsfield, Crippen, Bobko, Fullerton.
Source: CSNR Reference Collection.

MOL group 2 astronauts.
From left to right:
Crippen, Overmyer,
Bobko, Fullerton, Hartsfield.
Source: CSNR Reference Collection.

Karol J. Bobko.
Source: CSNR Reference Collection.

Karol Joseph Bobko was born on 23 December 1937 in New York City. Bobko attended the prestigious Brooklyn Technical High School in New York before becoming a member of the first class to graduate from the Air Force Academy in 1959. Right out of the Academy, Bobko received his commission and navigator rating, then attended pilot training at Bartow Air Base in Florida and Vance Air Base in Oklahoma. Bobko completed his training and received his wings in 1960.[53] For the next five years, Bobko recalled, "I went into flying fighters. I had the bug of getting into space probably because there were quite a few instructors when I was back at the Academy who used to tell us that this program they're starting, it won't be too long before we have people flying in space. So I flew fighters for a while."[54] In 1965, Bobko attended the Aerospace Research Test Pilot School at Edwards Air Force Base and was selected for MOL directly after graduation in 1966.

Robert L. Crippen.
Source: CSNR Reference Collection.

On 11 September 1937, Robert Laurel Crippen was born in Beaumont, Texas. Crippen graduated with a degree in aerospace engineering from the University of Texas in 1960, intending to become a pilot. Crippen joined the Navy and was commissioned through the U.S. Navy's Aviation Officer Candidate School, completing flight training in 1962.[55] For the next two years, he served as an attack pilot, explaining, "I served a tour in the Navy, mostly operating in the Mediterranean off the aircraft carrier *Independence*."[56] Next, as Crippen recalled, "I applied for Test Pilot School in the Navy and Air Force exchange, and I ended up at the Air Force Test Pilot School at Edwards Air Force Base – that was 1965. While I was there, both NASA and the military requested applicants for astronauts. I applied and when I ended up having to decide, I decided to go with MOL because NASA was already cutting back, and they had lots of astronauts on board, so I thought the best chance of flying was with the military."[57]

Charles G. Fullerton.
Source: CSNR Reference Collection.

Charles Gordon Fullerton was born in Rochester, New York on 11 October 1936. Fullerton's family moved to Portland, Oregon when he was young, and he graduated from high school there. Fullerton graduated with his bachelor's degree in mechanical engineering in 1957 from the California Institute of Technology in Pasadena. While getting his master's in mechanical engineering at Cal Tech, Fullerton worked as a mechanical design engineer in the Flight Test Department for Hughes Aircraft in Culver City. He graduated in July 1958 and joined the Air Force. Fullerton attended flight school, and he was trained as an F-86 interceptor pilot and eventually a B-47 bomber pilot. In 1964, Fullerton made a life-changing decision and attended the Air Force's ARPS at Edwards. After graduation, he reported to Wright-Patterson Air Force Base in Ohio as a bomber test pilot and was stationed there when he was selected for MOL.[58]

Henry W. Hartsfield.
Source: CSNR Reference Collection.

Robert F. Overmyer.
Source: CSNR Reference Collection.

The oldest of the second group, Henry Warren Hartsfield, Jr. was born in Birmingham, Alabama on 21 November 1933. A Reserve Officer Training Corps (ROTC) student, Hartsfield studied physics at Auburn University, graduating in 1954. Hartsfield joined the Air Force following graduation and became a pilot. He was stationed in Bitburg, Germany briefly and returned to the U.S. to attend ARPS at Edwards. Hartsfield remained at Edwards as an instructor in the school until he was selected for MOL in 1966. Macleay recalled Hartsfield's days as an instructor, "He developed Maxwell's equations from the start. That's all I needed, was to sit there and watch. He was smart as a whip."[59]

Robert Franklin Overmyer was the only member of the Marine Corps selected for MOL. He was born on 14 July 1936 in Lorain, Ohio, although he grew up in neighboring Westlake, located on the banks of Lake Erie. An avid outdoorsman and adventurer, Overmyer studied physics at Baldwin Wallace College in Berea, Ohio, graduating in 1958. Overmyer joined the Marine Corps in January 1958 and completed his Navy flight training in Kingsville, Texas. From 1959 to 1962, Overmyer served with the Marine Attack Squadron. In 1962, Overmyer enrolled in the Naval Post Graduate School, graduating in 1964 with a master's degree in aeronautics. He spent the next year with Marine Maintenance Squadron 17 in Iwakuni, Japan before he returned to the U.S. to attend ARPS at Edwards, where he was selected for MOL in 1966.[60]

Selecting the Third Group

Similar to the second group, the third group of pilots had a better idea of what they were applying for than did the first. James Abrahamson recalled, "We knew that the test pilot class, we had been selected as potential MOL astronauts in a test, in a competitive selection. About half of that test pilot school was made up of potential MOL selectees. Then depending on how well we performed in the test pilot class, we were selected over some who were not selected to move forward."[61] Although they knew they were being selected for MOL, they still did not have the information to grasp the scope of the program. Abrahamson stated, "I had no understanding at all of our satellite surveillance program."[62]

In May 1967, the MOL Astronaut Selection Board met to select the third increment of astronauts from the eight candidates that remained of the 25 initially nominated to the MOL Director in early 1966.[63] The board met 11-12 May 1967 and recommended that of the eight candidates, four should be selected for the program – James A. Abrahamson, Robert T. Herres, Robert H. Lawrence, Jr., and Donald H. Peterson.[64] One year after the announcement of the second group, Major Robert Hermann

MOL group 3 astronauts. From left to right: Herres, Lawrence, Peterson, Abrahamson.
Source: CSNR Reference Collection.

of the MOL Program Office announced the third group of new MOL astronauts on Friday, 30 June 1967, at a low-key press conference in Los Angeles.[65] The third group was quickly read into the program, given assignments, and became integrated members of the program.

The Third Group of MOL Pilots

At 34 years of age when he was selected for MOL, James Alan Abrahamson had already accomplished a great deal. Abrahamson was born on 19 May 1933 in Williston, North Dakota but grew up in Inglewood, California. He attended the Massachusetts Institute of Technology and graduated with a degree in aeronautical engineering in 1955. Following graduation, Abrahamson was commissioned a second lieutenant through the ROTC program and attended his pilot training at Laughlin Air Force Base in Texas, completing it in May 1957. For the next two years, he served as a flight instructor at Bryan Air Force Base in Texas. He then pursued further education and graduated with a master's degree in aerospace engineering from the University of Oklahoma in 1961. In August 1961, Abrahamson was transferred to the VELA Nuclear Detection Satellite Program at Los Angeles Air Force Station in California. It was Abrahamson's first space program, and he explained that he worked on the portion known as "Vela Hotel for Vela High Altitude. That was

James A. Abrahamson.
Source: CSNR Reference Collection.

the development of a group of dedicated satellites for this mission which were to be launched on Atlas rockets."⁶⁶ From 1964 to 1965, Abrahamson served two tours of duty in Southeast Asia, flying 49 combat missions, while assigned to a tactical fighter squadron out of Cannon Air Base in New Mexico. Next, Abrahamson attended the Air Command and Staff College, finishing as a distinguished graduate in July 1966. He continued to pursue his education and attended ARPS at Edwards, where he was selected for the third group of pilots for MOL.⁶⁷

Robert T. Herres.
Source: CSNR Reference Collection.

Robert Tralles Herres was born on 1 December 1932 in Denver, Colorado. He graduated from the U.S. Naval Academy in Annapolis, Maryland in 1954 and chose to serve in the Air Force rather than pursue a career in the Navy. Herres attended flight training at Webb Air Force Base in Texas and became an interceptor pilot. From 1955 to 1958, Herres served as a pilot and electronics maintenance officer with a fighter interceptor squadron stationed at Kirtland Air Force Base near Albuquerque, New Mexico. In 1959, Herres began attending the Air Force Institute of Technology and graduated with his master's degree in electrical engineering in 1960. Following graduation, he transferred to Lindsey Air Base in Germany where he served as an intelligence officer, and later as a flight training supervisor with the U.S. European Command Electronic Intelligence Center. Returning to the U.S. in 1964, Herres enrolled at the Air Command and Staff College at Maxwell Air Force Base, graduating in 1965. Herres was busy with his education, graduating with a master's in public administration from George Washington University also in 1965. Herres remained at Maxwell, serving as an instructor at the Air War College in weapons employment planning the following year, until he transferred to Edwards Air Force Base to attend ARPS. While attending ARPS, Herres was selected for MOL in 1967.⁶⁸

Robert H. Lawrence, Jr..
Source: CSNR Reference Collection.

Talented and brilliant, Robert Henry Lawrence, Jr. was the first African American selected for spaceflight. He was born on 2 October 1935 in Chicago where he graduated from Englewood High School at the age of 16. Lawrence then attended Bradley University in Peoria, Illinois, graduating with a degree in chemistry in 1956 at age 20. Upon graduation, Lawrence was commissioned a second lieutenant in the Air Force and attended pilot training at Malden Air Force Base in Missouri. Following training, Lawrence served until 1961 as a fighter pilot and instructor, stationed at Furstenfeldbruck Air Force Base near Munich in West Germany. Returning to the U.S., Lawrence entered the Air Force Institute of Technology at Wright-Patterson Air Force Base and later was assigned as a nuclear research officer at Kirtland Air Force Base. Lawrence continued to pursue his education and graduated from Ohio State University in 1965 with his PhD in nuclear chemistry. In June 1967, Lawrence completed his training at ARPS at Edwards and was selected for MOL, earning him the designation as the first selected African American astronaut.

Only six months later, in a tragic accident, Lawrence was killed during a training flight on 8 December 1967 in an F-104 aircraft crash at Edwards Air Force Base. Lawrence was flying in the backseat, serving as an instructor pilot for a flight test trainee learning the challenging but essential steep-descent glide landing technique. During landing, the plane hit the ground hard, and the plane

Donald H. Peterson.
Source: CSNR Reference Collection.

rolled and caught fire. Although the pilot successfully ejected upward and survived the crash, Lawrence's back seat ejected to the side and he was killed instantly. Lawrence achieved much in his short 32 years, and he would undoubtedly have gone on to achieve considerable success.[69]

Donald Herod Peterson was born in Winona, Mississippi on 22 October 1933. Peterson graduated from the U.S. Military Academy at West Point, New York in 1955 and elected to join the Air Force. Following pilot training, Peterson served as an Air Training Command instructor and military training officer until 1960. Peterson returned to school and graduated with a master's degree in nuclear engineering from the Air Force Institute of Technology at Wright-Patterson Air Force Base in 1962. For the next five years, Peterson served as a nuclear systems analyst with the Air Force Systems Command and as a fighter pilot with the Tactical Air Command. Peterson graduated from ARPS at Edwards prior to being selected for MOL in 1967.[70]

By all recollections, all three crew selections formed a tight-knit group. Abrahamson fondly reminisced, "It was cohesive, and we all had different responsibilities."[71] Truly explained, "It was very close. I mean, in any group of human beings, you're going to like somebody more than another and enjoy working with somebody more than another. But everybody worked like hell. My recollection, I didn't see a lot of acrimonious behavior at all. It was interesting because eventually we had three crew selections, and we had a couple of people leave… But over the three selections, we ended up having 14 people in the flight crew office. And they were a very interesting set of people. One of them went on to be Vice Chairman of the Joint Chiefs, the first one. Between us we had flown many different kinds of airplanes. And we flew a lot, we trained together. It was a fun time, it really was. I really loved it."[72] The group was not only cohesive, but it was also impressive. Macleay recalled, "The flight crew was an amazing bunch of people, as far as I was concerned. You look back, and you're going to work every day with guys like Dick Truly and Bob Crippen and Hank Hartsfield and Larry Skantze and Bob Herres and Jim Abrahamson. Good Lord. If you can't pick something up, just by osmosis, being around those kinds of people, you've got to be stupid… You just can't be around those kinds of excellent people without learning something."[73]

Fourteen of the Seventeen selected MOL astronauts. From left to right, top row: Herres, Hartsfield, Overmyer, Fullerton, Crippen, Peterson, Bobko, Abrahamson. From left to right, bottom row: Finley, Lawyer, Taylor, Crews, Neubeck, Truly.
Source: CSNR Reference Collection.

Endnotes

1. Oral History interview with Lachlan Macleay, 2 June 2014, p. 5, CSNR/RC.
2. Oral History Interview with Richard Truly, 4 June 2014, p. 4, CSNR/RC.
3. Panel Discussion with Richard Truly, MOL Declassification Event at Dayton, Ohio, 22 October 2015.
4. Oral History Interview with Lachlan Macleay, 2 June 2014, p. 4, CSNR/RC.
5. Ibid, p. 5.
6. Ibid.
7. Ibid.
8. Oral History Interview with Lachlan Macleay, 2 June 2014, p. 6, CSNR/RC.
9. Ibid.
10. Policy Relating to Manned Orbiting Laboratory (MOL) Astronauts, 23 December 1966, NROARC. Memorandum for the Director (MOL), Flax, Sub: Policy Relating to MOL Astronauts, 28 December 1966, Job 199700050-02-008-015, NROARC.
11. Oral History Interview with Albert Crews, 24 March 2014, p. 4, CSNR/RC.
12. Ibid, p. 5.
13. Oral History Interview with Lachlan Macleay, 2 June 2014, p. 4, CSNR/RC.
14. Oral History Interview with Richard Truly, 4 June 2014, p. 4, CSNR/RC.
15. Oral History Interview with James Abrahamson, 20 June 2013, p.4, CSNR/RC.
16. Oral History Interview with Richard Truly, 4 June 2014, p. 5, CSNR/RC.
17. Panel Discussion with Richard Truly, MOL Declassification Event at Dayton, Ohio, 22 October 2015.
18. Memorandum, Schriever to Secretary of the Air Force, Sub: MOL Monthly Status Report for October 1965, 8 November 1965, Job 199700033-08-024-002, NROARC.
19. Memorandum, E. B. LeBailly (Director of Information), Sub: Annex 1, Manned Orbiting Laboratory (MOL) Information Plan, 11 June 1966, Job 199700057-01-002-012, NROARC.
20. Oral History interview with Lachlan Macleay, 2 June 2014, p. 7, CSNR/RC.
21. Memorandum, E. B. LeBailly (Director of Information), Sub: Annex 1, Manned Orbiting Laboratory (MOL) Information Plan, 11 June 1966, Job 199700057-01-002-012, NROARC.
22. Oral History Interview with Richard Truly, 4 June 2014, p. 5, CSNR/RC.
23. Michael Cassutt, *Who's Who in Space*, (New York: MacMillan Publishing Company, 1993), p. 192; Internet Web Site http://www.hq.nasa.gov/office/pao/History/x15/adams.html.
24. Oral History Interview with Albert Crews, 24 March 2014, p. 3, CSNR/RC.
25. Ibid.
26. Ibid, p. 11.
27. Cassutt, *Who's Who in Space, p. 205*.
28. Internet Web Site http://arlingtoncemetery.net/relawyer.htm. Cassutt, *Who's Who in Space, p. 206-7*.
29. Oral History Interview with Lachlan Macleay, 2 June 2014, p. 3, CSNR/RC.
30. Ibid.
31. Ibid.
32. Ibid.

33 Ibid, p.4.

34 Cassutt, *Who's Who in Space*, p. 207-8.

35 Ibid, p. 208.

36 Oral History Interview with Richard Truly, 4 June 2014, p. 3, CSNR/RC.

37 Ibid.

38 Ibid.

39 Ibid, p. 4.

40 Oral History Interview with Robert Crippen, 24 March 2014, p. 3, CSNR/RC.

41 Oral History interview with Robert Crippen, 24 March 2014, p. 3, CSNR/RC.

42 Ibid, p. 4.

43 Oral History Interview with Karol Bobko, 3 April 2014, p. 4, CSNR/RC.

44 Memorandum, Evans and Schriever to Secretary of the Air Force, Sub: MOL Monthly Status Report for June, 8 July 1966, Job 199700033-08-025F, NROARC.

45 Oral History Interview with Robert Crippen, 24 March 2014, p. 4, CSNR/RC.

46 Oral History Interview with Karol Bobko, 3 April 2014, p. 4, CSNR/RC.

47 Ibid, p. 10.

48 Oral History Interview with Albert Crews, 24 March 2014, p. 6, CSNR/RC.

49 Memorandum, Schriever to Secretary of the Air Force, Sub: MOL Monthly Status Report for December, 4 January 1966, Job 199700033-08-026A, NROARC.

50 Ibid.

51 Memorandum, Evans and Schriever to Secretary of the Air Force, Sub: MOL Monthly Status Report for April, 6 May 1966, Job 199700033-08-026E, NROARC.

52 Memorandum, E. B. LeBailly (Director of Information), Sub: Annex 1, Manned Orbiting Laboratory (MOL) Information Plan, 11 June 1966, Job 199700057-01-002-012, NROARC.

53 Internet Web Site http://www.jsc.nasa.gov/Bios/htmlbios/bobko-kj.html.

54 Oral History Interview with Karol Bobko, 3 April 2014, p. 3, CSNR/RC.

55 Cassutt, *Who's Who in Space*, p. 44.

56 Oral History Interview with Robert Crippen, 24 March 2014, p. 3, CSNR/RC.

57 Oral History Interview with Robert Crippen, 24 March 2014, p. 3, CSNR/RC.

58 Internet Web Site http://www.jsc.nasa.gov/Bios/htmlbios/fullerton-cg.html; Internet Web Site http://www.nytimes.com/2013/08/23/us/c-gordon-fullerton-early-space-shuttle-pilot-dies-at-76.html?_r=0 Charles Gordon Fullerton; Cassutt, *Who's Who in Space*, p. 54.

59 Oral History Interview with Lachlan Macleay, 2 June 2014, p. 4, CSNR/RC.

60 Internet Web Site http://www.jsc.nasa.gov/Bios/htmlbios/overmyer.html; Cassutt, *Who's Who in Space*, p. 99.

61 Oral History Interview with James Abrahamson, 20 June 2013, p. 4, CSNR/RC.

62 Ibid.

63 Memorandum, Stewart and Ferguson to Secretary of the Air Force, Sub: MOL Monthly Status Report for April, 5 May 1967, Job 199700033-08-027G, NROARC.

64 Memorandum, Stewart to Secretary of the Air Force, Sub: MOL Monthly Status Report for May, 5 June 1967, Job 199700033-08-027H, NROARC.

65. Memorandum, Stewart and Ferguson to Secretary of the Air Force, Sub: MOL Monthly Status Report for June, 6 July 1967, Job 199700033-08-028A, NROARC.

66. Ibid.

67. Internet Web Site http://www.af.mil/AboutUs/Biographies/Display/tabid/225/Article/107876/lieutenant-general-james-a-abrahamson.aspx; Cassutt, *Who's Who in Space, p. 204.*

68. Internet Web Site http://www.af.mil/AboutUs/Biographies/Display/tabid/225/Article/106789/general-robert-t-herres.aspx; Cassutt, *Who's Who in Space, p. 205-6.*

69. Internet Web Site http://www.hill.af.mil/library/factsheets/factsheet.asp?id=5878; Internet Web Site http://www.raahistory.com/military/airforce/lawrence/lawrence.htm; Cassutt, *Who's Who in Space, p. 206.*

70. Internet Web Site http://www.jsc.nasa.gov/Bios/htmlbios/peterson-dh.html; Cassutt, *Who's Who in Space, p. 100-101.*

71. Oral History Interview with James Abrahamson, 20 June 2013, p. 14, CSNR/RC.

72. Oral History Interview with Richard Truly, 4 June 2014, p. 9, CSNR/RC.

73. Oral History Interview with Lachlan Macleay, 2 June 2014, p. 19, CSNR/RC.

Chapter 3

MOL UP AND RUNNING

With fourteen exceptional pilots selected to man MOL, the program began to take shape. From the beginning, rigorous engineering challenges and training exercises prepared the MOL astronauts to tackle the unknown of space reconnaissance. As a group, building on individuals' strengths, the astronauts developed a concept that would maximize the presence of man and offer relevant, groundbreaking reconnaissance. Meanwhile, the pilots also participated in rigorous training exercises to prepare them for what was to come.

Integrating Man

Although the U.S. had successfully launched and used satellites in secret for years by the time MOL was up and running, the incorporation of man into a reconnaissance program introduced a new set of security concerns. In response, policies regulating the crew members were put in place immediately upon their selection. By October 1965, General Schriever had approved a directive regulating crew member activity, the intent of which was to prevent any glamorizing of crew member status and activity.[1] Under the policy, all crew members were assigned to the MOL Systems Office and were to be treated like all other officer personnel assigned to the program. Crew members were to be referred to as "crew member" rather than "astronaut." Further, public information would be strictly limited. Crew members were not to publish articles or make public appearances or speeches. They were directed not to respond to any questions from the media or public. No information regarding crew schedules and training was to be released to anyone outside the program.[2]

MOL program patch.
Source: CSNR Reference Collection.

Those involved were excited to discover what man could contribute. But even after program approval and selection of the crew members, it still was not entirely clear what the crew members themselves would be doing. When asked about the goals of the program as a whole, Karol Bobko stated, "The main goals for the MOL program were going to be to get high resolution photography and to get some data, operational experience in the space arena."[3] Initially he thought the pilots would be conducting "experiments undefined, kind of like Skylab where you have a spacecraft which has capabilities… There wasn't any specific focus like there was later on in the MOL."[4] Similarly, Crippen recalled that the main goal of the program was photoreconnaissance. Additionally, he stated that there were other "unclassified things about how well could humans work in space, live long-term – long-term was 30 days at that time. There were those kinds of objectives as well."[5] The hope was that MOL would discover and demonstrate unknown uses for man in space. In a December 1965 memorandum, the NRO Staff's Chief Security Officer Louis Mazza described MOL in these terms: "Notwithstanding the fact that MOL was justified based upon a requirement for improved high resolution photography, MOL is still essentially a manned orbiting laboratory. One of the most significant factors it will demonstrate is man's ability to perform designated, militarily useful tasks in space for periods up to 30 days operating in a shirt-sleeve environment."[6]

With minimal fanfare, the crew members were brought on to the program and given assignments. Macleay recalled that after getting clearances, "We then started around a few trips. Some of us went down to McDonnell Douglas down in Huntington Beach where they were going to build the mounted capsule. We went to McDonnell Douglas who was flying the Gemini and General Electric who was doing a lot of the work. That's kind of it. Then we got started."[7] Each crew member eventually found his own niche, and there was plenty to do. Macleay reflected, "What was the routine? Well the routine was you kind of did what had to be done at the time. There was very seldom where you ever just punched in a clock, going in and coming out, because you're always on the road, you're up at Sunnyvale or you're at the Control Center… I don't think there was ever a dull moment, nobody was ever really bored on the program. There was always something to do."[8]

Individual Roles

As the program evolved, crew members took on different responsibilities. Truly explained, "The way the flight crew office worked… is that every crewman who is in training and hoping to fly is assigned to some technological job in the office. In our case, one person would work spacesuits or one would work the Gemini capsule or one would work various systems, that kind of a thing."[9] Similarly, Abrahamson recalled, "Some were selected to work on an EVA suit… Others were working on other parts of the training program."[10] With crew members spread out across contractors and tasks, the program required regular coordination. Crews remembered, "We tried to have a group meeting every Monday starting off the week to go over what everybody was going to be doing that week. We usually had two guys working together. [In the beginning] there were the eight of us, so that was four different groups. Probably half of us would still be there in the office, and the other four would be traveling somewhere."[11] Crippen explained, "We were busy doing engineering kind of work. We'd have our regular pilot meetings once a week to share what we knew was going on."[12]

The crew members were generally assigned, often in pairs, to work with a contractor on a specific portion of the program, which also required coordination. Bobko explained, "Typically you had a contractor who was going to be doing some part of the activity, whatever it happened to be. For instance, McDonnell was doing the laboratory, and Douglas was doing the Gemini… Typically you'd have a contractor, you had contract administration, then you had some technical people, Air Force usually, who oversaw what was happening there. Then you had some Aerospace guys, typically, who were the engineers who were helping what needed to be done."[13] Each piece – the contractor, the Aerospace engineers, the Air Force oversight, the crew members – worked together and coordinated in order to accomplish the monumental amount of work. Coordinating with contractors required a significant amount of travel. Macleay explained, "We were taking a lot of trips. Lots of times we would be driving down to meetings at McDonnell Douglas down in Huntington Beach or we'd be flying into Valley Forge or we'd be going to McDonnell Douglas at St. Louis. We traveled quite a bit, sometimes under funny circumstances. I think when we went to Rochester up there to see the big flats being made and all that stuff, that was all, 'Don't tell anybody where you're going.'"[14]

Crew members were assigned to and provided crew input on all aspects of the program. Some crew members helped develop a MOL flight suit. The suit was similar to the Apollo suit in design, but by incorporating a hip-waist joint, it allowed for increased mobility and self-donning and doffing.[15] Recalling his own assignment, Crippen stated, "The crew was each given particular areas to go work on and follow, put in crew input, controls in this place. I worked very hard with Douglas on the controls for the laboratory. We were building a simulator at General Electric to be able to do some of the training for the classified work. I worked on that as well."[16] Many crew members worked closely with others on specific projects. Crippen recalled, "Dick Truly was another Navy guy, he and I shared an office. We were both working on simulations that I mentioned."[17] Meanwhile Crews felt like he "was more of an office worker than any of the other guys. We had kind of broken up the guys assigned to certain things."[18] As he remembered it, although people were assigned to various pieces of the program, "we would kind of help each other out as we went."[19]

According to Crews, Richard Lawyer spent his time "riding on all the zero-G flights" and working the tunnel between the Gemini B capsule and the laboratory module.[20] Crippen explained further that both "Dick Lawyer and Bob Overmyer did some work in the zero-gravity airplane, the KC-135, with suits, seeing whether they could get in and out of certain things. Normally the method for getting from the Gemini to the lab was through a hatch and going back into it. But there was a backup mode of actually going EVA to do a transfer back and get into the Gemini. So there were people working on that kind of stuff."[21]

MOL spacesuit. Source: CSNR Reference Collection.

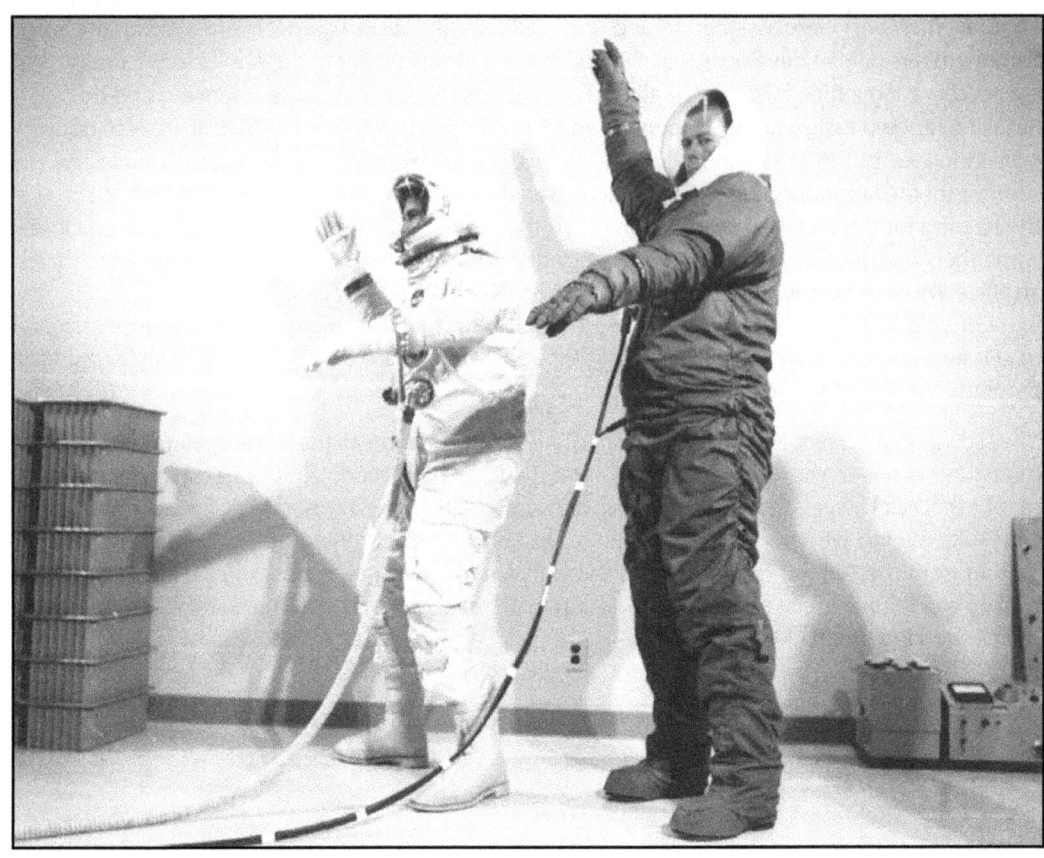

Practicing movement in the MOL spacesuit.
Source: CSNR Reference Collection.

There was some concern about the feasibility of navigating the tunnel between the Gemini capsule and the laboratory module. Crews recalled, "It was a challenge to be able to climb from the Gemini back through an 18-inch hole into the laboratory. Then later on, you had to come back the other way, and both times you were in a pressure suit doing that. We trained for it, and of course all of us didn't do it. But two guys, going through the hole, did do it on the zero-G airplane the best it could be done. Of course all the rest of us knew that if those guys could do it, we could do it."[22]

Of his work, Bobko recalled, "I worked as a crew member who worked with engineers in a couple of the systems on board, specifically the reaction controls, the orbital control, the maneuvering control system."[23] As a crew member, he was able to offer valuable insight during the design process. More specifically, he explained, "If you talk about the little maneuvering rockets that are on the spacecraft, I was really a part of the team, with a couple of Aerospace guys and a couple of Air Force guys, that were working with the contractors to try to get this stuff. They may come and say, 'From a crew perspective, what do you think about this sequence of how you control this? Or these, however this is, this is what we're going to do with the displays.'"[24] Eventually, if the program had gone further, Bobko stated, "I was supposed to be working with the folks who were looking at measuring man's contribution to the MOL mission."[25]

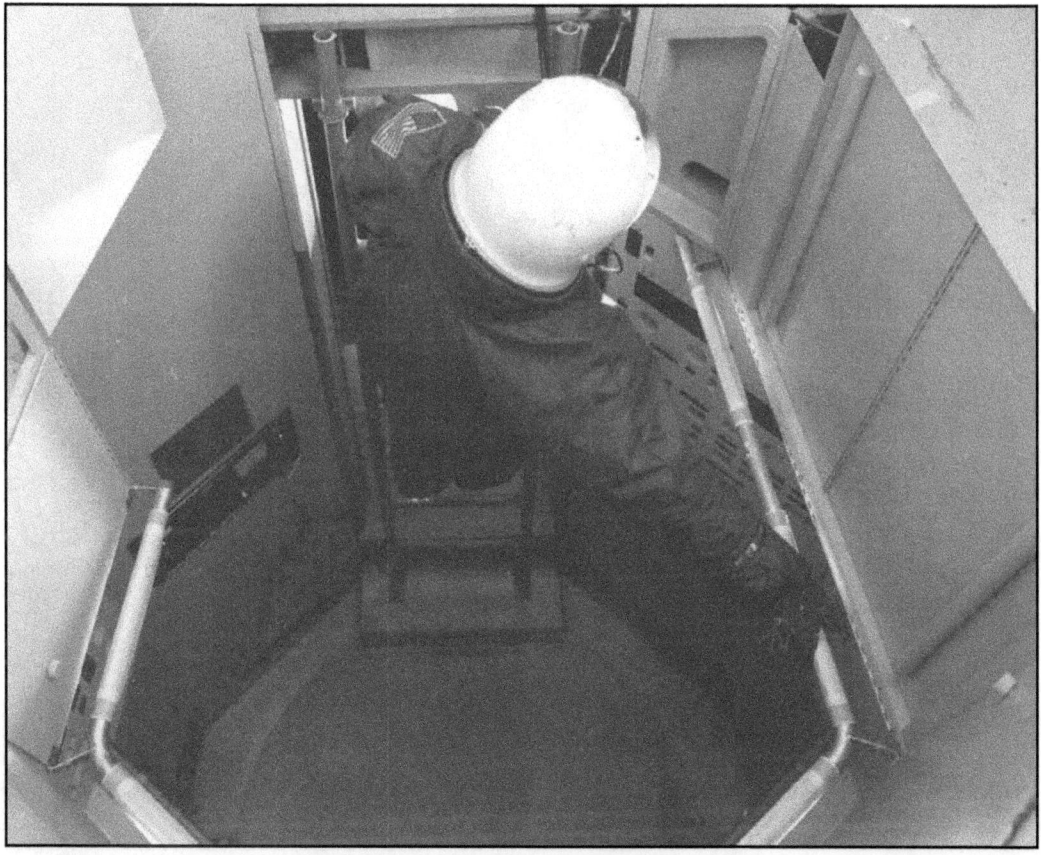

Practicing moving through the MOL tunnel.
Source: CSNR Reference Collection.

A New Concept For Man

There was some flexibility within assignments, and many of the crew members worked within their areas of expertise and interest. Truly recalled, "I was interested in the mission, the targeting, and so I gravitated to work in that area. And so did Mac Macleay... As the program went on, that's what we did on behalf of the flight crew."[26] Crews recalled, "As I remember, Macleay and Truly were the head guys regarding software. At that time software was a new profession."[27] Exploring man's role in targeting and better defining the mission, Truly and Macleay worked on what became the centerpiece of MOL. Bobko recollected, "The program went along, and there wasn't terribly good definition of the mission. Then I think it was Truly and Macleay [who] were the ones who really dreamed it up."[28] Truly reflected, "Eventually we developed not just a concept, but a set of hardware and procedures so that we knew what we were going to do."[29]

The main goal of the program was to attain high resolution reconnaissance photography, so how did man fit into that? Macleay explained that their concept "became kind of the basis for the manned interface and how we were going to help select targets. We actually had two things to do: one was image motion compensation to get the best resolution you could get. The other was target selection."[30] Both crew members were essential. Truly explained, "You had a commander and a pilot... Once we got on orbit, it was strictly a team operation. Both guys had to know how to do everything."[31] Bobko explained the basic idea for target selection, "What they did was add basically a couple of spotting scopes on the main [telescope]... What they were going to have us do is they were going to put a

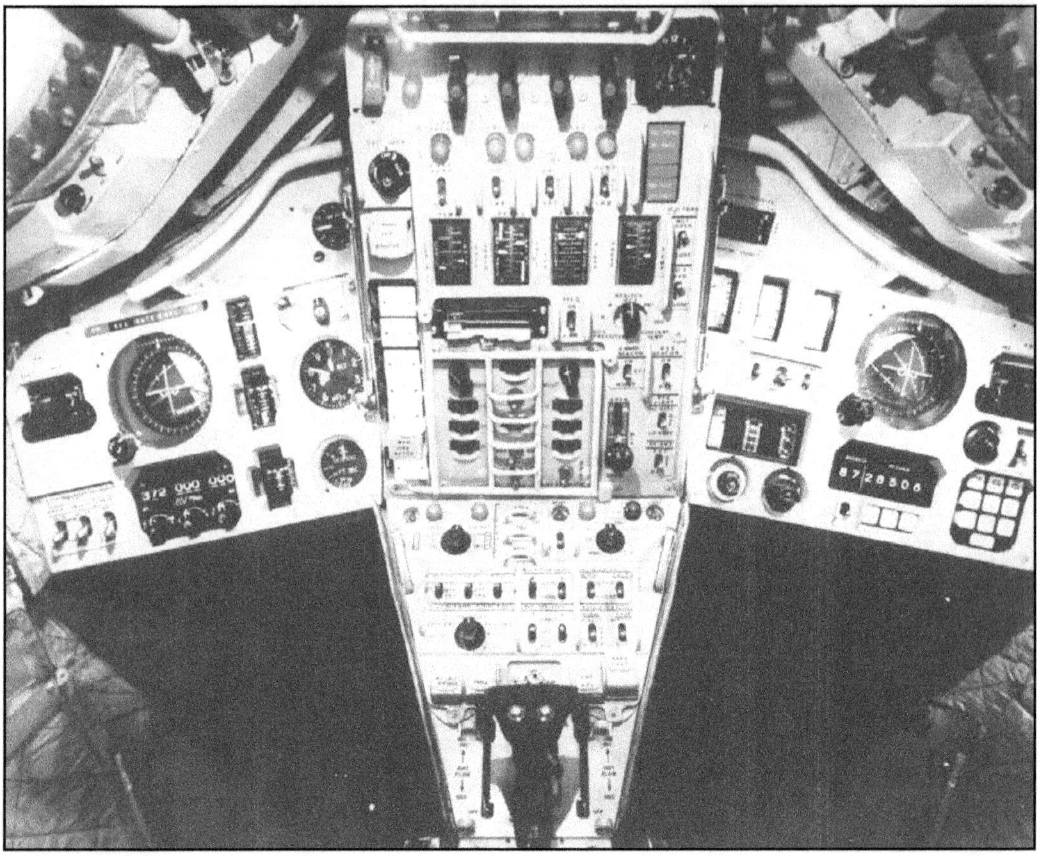

Flight control panel. Source: CSNR Reference Collection.

Simulated control panel for training. Source: CSNR Reference Collection.

little, small telescope that would have a quick response, the crew could use one of these. [It] would be programmed to go to the tentative sites they were going to photograph with the large telescope. Then you would vote among those."[32] Truly explained further, "We developed a concept and then a capability [for the] two crew. If they were going over a target area, we had two telescopes that were high-powered telescopes. I don't remember what resolution they were, but [they] could jump from potential target to potential target."[33] Looking ahead to potential sites, the crew members were given the capability to avoid bad weather and identify activity at potential sites of interest.

Prior to flight, targets were divided into three categories: primary targets which were mandatory if any activity were present, alternate targets which were optional targets based on weather and activity, and visual intelligence targets which were targets that were preselected for crew inspection and commentary but not photos.[34] Macleay explained the process this way, "Of course all the targets are loaded from the ground, they all have their own priorities. Left to its own devices, the system would just go from highest priority to highest priority all the way through. We had developed a system where we could input [priority]... We had activity indicators: this target is active and that would affect its priority. If, for instance, you were going over a missile silo field and the thing honed in on a silo with the lid shut and the next one had the lid open, well the lid open was more important than the lid shut because you might see something. We were developing activity indicators using the Gambit product, looking at things and saying, 'Now that didn't necessarily say that was going to be the target selected.' But we would say, 'Hey, this one is active,' and it could affect its priority in the machine itself. Or if it was covered with weather, you could say, 'Not worth taking a picture, all you're going to see is a cloud.'"[35] Over the course of a single day, MOL would orbit earth several times, allowing the crew to continue adapting to changing situations. Bobko explained, "It would be just the two crew members. You know that there are going to be a number of passes in the day when you're going to be probably having a bunch of tentative targets over or around Moscow, etc."[36]

As a developer of the concept, Macleay also had to help sell it. In July 1967, Macleay briefed officials, including the Vice President, on the role of the flight crew during MOL orbital operations.[37] He recalled, "Then I was the guy that got to brief the Chief of Staff of the Air Force on the operational concept. I got to brief the President's scientific advisory board with Hubert Humphrey the morning after the Detroit riots [28 July 1968], along with Dick Helms, the head of the CIA, and all those people... I got to brief them on the operational concept. That was kind of funny because they have a huge screen and, as a pointer, they gave me a fly rod with a little light on the end of it. Have you ever tried to hold it? I was a little nervous to start with, never having been in front of the Vice President or Dick Helms or those guys before. But everybody afterwards said, 'You sure couldn't hold that thing steady up there.' You try!"[38]

With the concept in place, Truly and Macleay worked to integrate it into a functional system. Truly explained, "Then we had to develop a software program so that, for example, if the telescope would slew to a launch pad, you would have just a few seconds to decide, 'Is it cloud covered? Is there a missile on the pad? Is there something of great interest or no interest? Is it empty?' And make an input in just a few seconds as to what the value of that particular target was. Then the telescope would slew to another target."[39] The idea was that after the crew had inspected the potential target, they were given four optional computer inputs: reject, inactive, active, or override in cases of unusually high intelligence value.[40] For example, Truly explained, "If you were say going over to Europe and you had all the Soviet launch pads, maybe the telescope was preprogrammed to dwell on the first one, then the second one, then the third one, then the fourth one. And in each case, the crewman would look at it with his own eyes and make a judgment as to what kind of interest that was to the intelligence community. It was fascinating work because you had to learn about what was of interest. And then you get to make input about whether or not you thought that image, if the system took it, would be of great value or no value. Then we had to develop a program that took all of these inputs and actually targeted the main imaging system at the highest value target. It was a very complex, real-time computer program that was required to take either one or two crewmen's inputs and take all these inputs about high-value and clouds, whatever, and actually target the system to take the highest value targets. And that's the way the system was designed to be worked. We were unsuccessful for a long time, but in the late spring of 1969, Eureka, we had it! We had it."[41]

> "...in the late spring of 1969, Eureka, we had it! We had it."

The Role of the Astronaut

In this model for the MOL, the crew would work together to ensure more efficient and effective use of film, avoiding cloud cover and inactive targets – an exciting opportunity for the crew to contribute. Abrahamson explained, "There are two telescopes that were not really high performance telescopes. They were to be able to do sighting ahead of the MOL, as it's moving in orbit. We were to make inputs so that we could decide what targets were cloud-covered, which had any indicator of activity. That's the real issue. We would vote, and the intent was to be able to have every photograph be as high of value as possible. It was, I thought, a great experiment on optimizing what a human being, working in a robotic environment, could do. Really, really exciting."[42] This concept was new, innovative, and unique to MOL. Bobko stated, "To me that was one of the things that was most important about [MOL], was to use the crew to go ahead and filter out a lot of these places so you didn't take pictures of them, you didn't waste film."[43] Truly and Macleay were essential to developing this core concept. Truly fondly reminisced, "We were at the heart of MOL. I mean that was the very core of why we were going to fly."[44]

Others in the program worked to make this new concept feasible. Abrahamson, who joined the program in 1967, explained, "My job was to build a very complex simulator with some really advanced optics because you might be looking out at the side at a high angle at this thing where the next orbit you may be over here looking at a different angle… It's a very complex training test. And defining what activity is. Are there people out there or just some guys drinking vodka off in the corner? Or is there really an airplane there or something like it? It was an exciting mission. That's why I say it was this combination of what a human flash judgment might be able to bring and putting that into this highly automated system."[45] Adequate training for crew members was absolutely essential, especially given the fast pace: they were to evaluate as many targets as possible in 15-25 seconds.[46] It was critical that crew members become experts in near instantaneous evaluation of virtually every type of target.[47] All told, the concept, software, hardware, and training simulators were well on their way to being operational by the spring of 1969.

The system remained adaptable even with this new concept. Requirements called for a bimodal system configuration of both an automatic mode and a manned mode. In a memorandum regarding the new operations concept, the separate modes were explained, "There are two basic modes of operation for the manned/automatic vehicle configuration. Mode A is the automatic mode in which the mission payload and its subsystems are operating properly, and all target centering, image motion compensation (IMC), and photography are accomplished without crew assistance. The flight crew's functions in this mode range from enhancing the technical intelligence of the photography through the target selection process, to completely checking out the operation of the automatic systems. Mode B is the backup mode in which the crew is required to assist in centering, IMC, or other functions which the crew can perform, but which normally would be satisfactorily accomplished on computer command in Mode A. Mode B stresses continued use of all available automatic features that are operational."[48] With both manned and automatic modes available, the debate over the need for man plagued the program until the very end. However, many were convinced that this concept was essential. Bobko reflected, "To have a crew onboard, you could have somebody looking at what's happening and decide whether or not they want to take a photo or other data of whatever it is that you're watching... Selection of data, I think, is one of the big things, that you can have somebody knowledgeable look at this."[49]

Crew members and leadership continued to evolve and adapt the role of man in the program. Initially, program personnel conceived that man could help the system in target acquisition, centering, image motion compensation, and inspection and selection of alternate targets based on weather conditions.[50] The opportunities for contribution increased as the concept developed by Macleay and Truly gave man a unique role in detecting high value intelligence targets utilizing the added high resolution acquisition and tracking telescopes. Ultimately, man would be used in three separate and essential activities: to preserve the quantity and quality of photography, to preserve the effective spacecraft performance throughout the duration of the mission, and to develop knowledge on how crewmen improve the quality, quantity, and reliability of the mission through a variety of manned experiments on orbit.[51] Additionally, some envisioned that man could survey specific areas during crisis conditions, photograph other satellites, and conduct casual visual reconnaissance of a variety of targets.[52] One 1968 memorandum summarized man's contributions by stating that the role of the flight crew was "to enhance the quantity and quality of the photographic intelligence derived from the MOL/DORIAN flights" and "to aid in the rapid maturing of the system... while simultaneously gathering high-resolution photographic reconnaissance data."[53]

In a document titled "The Roles of Man in MOL" dated 1 June 1969 – only 9 days before the program was canceled – the program office argued, "Man has been included in the MOL system because his presence is necessary to guarantee successful accomplishment of program objectives."[54] In MOL, man was to be a pilot, systems manager and operator, engineer, diagnostician, experimenter, photographer and photo-interpreter, observer, reporter, and adviser on the future utility of man in military and scientific space missions.[55] The program office argued, "Man is a vital ingredient of the MOL system. His presence will ensure that the designated program objectives are achieved and that they will be achieved early and economically."[56] Those involved with the program believed that man's presence offered versatility, flexibility, and unknown opportunities for further exploitation and growth.

Additionally, man was absolutely critical to realizing the program goal of achieving superior photography. The program office stated, "It is clear that man can guarantee precision pointing to the accuracy required for achieving [superior] resolution photography... In short, man's presence guarantees virtually perfect pointing capability for the MOL system."[57] Highlighting Macleay and Truly's concept, the program office stated, "The most significant enhancement contribution probably will result from man's ability to verify 'activity' of high intelligence value at alternate locations."[58] Finally, in conclusion, program officials stated, "The MOL system has been designed for maximum operational capability through exploitation of the inherent attributes of man. Progress made to date, in refining the design of system hardware and software, in establishing operational procedures, etc., and in simulating the tasks he will be called upon to perform, reinforces the conviction that MOL will more than live up to the potential envisioned when man was originally incorporated into the system."[59]

Training the Crew

When asked about specific astronaut training for MOL crew members, Robert Crippen responded, "I would say that we never got into what I would call a 'training phase.' We were busy doing engineering kind of work… It wasn't training so much as it was assessing whether we could do some of the things we were being asked to do."[60] Indeed, the program was cut short in 1969 before anyone began mission-specific training. Yet in assessing the viability of some of the mission plan and technology, many crew members had the opportunity to participate in a variety of exciting and unique training exercises.

The MOL Program Office outlined four phases of training beginning with Phase I, or indoctrination, which was scheduled to last two months.[61] During indoctrination, crew members were to be "given general knowledge on all aspects of MOL" via briefings and site visits to both NASA and contractor facilities.[62] Phase II was a five-month training program at the Aerospace Research Pilots School at Edwards Air Force Base. During that training, crew members were to be provided "with technical courses related to MOL vehicle systems, operations procedures, and mission plans."[63] Crew members participated in classroom training, flights, and T-27 space simulator flights during Phase II. Crew members would spend most of their time in Phase III – the engineering development and crew integration phase. Phase III was a "continuous training effort throughout the remaining period of time before assignment to a flight" in which "each crew member is assigned an area of responsibility which he operationally and technically monitors and to which he provides crew inputs."[64] Any other "government agency, contractor, and other supported training" was also scheduled to be accomplished during Phase III.[65] Pre-Flight training, or Phase IV, was designed to be conducted after a crew member was assigned to a specific flight and for the twelve months leading up to the flight. The goal of the training was to prepare them to manage all parts of the MOL system – the Gemini B, the Laboratory Module, and the Mission Payload Module – and was to be conducted largely at the system simulator at Vandenberg Air Force Base.[66]

The MOL Program Plan called for eight separate training hardware items to be used over the course of program training. The Laboratory Module Simulation Equipment, the Mission Payload Simulation Equipment, and the Gemini B Procedures Simulator all prepared the crew members to interact with the various pieces of the MOL system. The Zero "G" Trainer was scheduled to be a series of simulations, including a C-135 flight and underwater training, to prepare crew members for the space environment, despite the mission module's depressurized design. The Abort Trainer was to prepare crew members in the event of a mission abort, and the Flotation-Egress Trainer was designed to prepare crew members for a water landing and "emergency escape in the event the spacecraft begins to leak."[67] The Centrifuge Trainer was designed to prepare crew members for powered flight while the last, the Development Simulator No. 2, was designed to prepare crew members in the operation of the mission segment.[68] Having trained on each simulator, crew members would be prepared in all elements of the system and equipped to manage a number of possible challenges or failures.

Much of the crew members' training fell within the parameters of Phase III, engineering development and crew integration, and involved days of study. Truly recalled, "It was long and hard, a lot of study. Of course the program was under development, so [training] was a lot of development. We would design panels and nomenclature and switches and interfaces. You had to design a head and the food system and all the things."[69] Crew members were integrally involved in the design, and it was critical that they understood every piece of the system. Bobko recalled that by 1968, "I had started doing things like training. You may be working some part of this program, but there are a lot of pieces, especially as a crew member, that you have to be knowledgeable about before you really start on the mission-specific training."⁷⁰ Crew members had been selected because they were bright and educated and had demonstrated their flight capabilities. Training, however, was about applying that knowledge to the program. Bobko explained, "There were just lots of things when you get into the spacecraft and space program that you start to learn that aren't necessarily taught to you in college courses."⁷¹ Training was about application of knowledge and simulations of the system.

Water Training

NASA-pioneered underwater training provided crew members with a neutrally buoyant environment in which to test and practice for the zero gravity environment of space. A member of the first group of pilots selected, Macleay recalled that a group "got scuba trained in Los Angeles itself, and then we all went out on the USC boat to Catalina and did scuba diving because we were going to do some water training later."⁷² Later in the program, after all three groups had been selected, Maj. Gen. Bleymaier asked crew members if they were scuba-certified. Abrahamson recalled that many were not, and Bleymaier instructed them, "Ok, go pick a school and get certified so I've got it on your record and if you get hurt, I can be blameless because I trained you."⁷³ Abrahamson remembered, "We all thought about that and one of the guys, a Navy guy, said, 'Well the Navy diving school, which is all sorts of diving including scuba, was down at Key West Florida.' So zingo! We all flew to Key West."⁷⁴

Key West was a memorable experience for all. Macleay recalled of the experience, "We went to the Navy's deep water school at Key West where we got all kinds of scuba training and diving bell training and Jacktar mask training and swimming and stuff, where they'd try to kill us while we got out of there."⁷⁵ A lighthearted interservice rivalry was evident as a group of Air Force officers attended the Navy dive school. Abrahamson recalled the Navy instructors "just delighted in going after us, especially the Air Force guys in this operation, but it was great fun."⁷⁶ Macleay described their final test in which Navy instructors tried to force students to surface. He recalled, "They'd knock your mask off. They'd rip the hose out of your mouth. They'd cut the hose. They finally got me up, but, good Lord, they knocked my mask off, cut the hose, turned off the tank… That was kind of fun."⁷⁷ With scuba training complete, a number of pilots traveled to Buck Island, located in the Virgin Islands, for training on a General Electric simulator. Crews recalled that several crew members "got to go down to the Virgin Islands with an underwater system that General Electric had put in" – remembering the experience to be "enjoyable."⁷⁸ Both Lawyer and Overmyer participated in additional zero-gravity simulation trainings at the Virgin Islands GE facility for a week in 1968.⁷⁹

Zero-gravity simulated underwater training.
Source: CSNR Reference Collection.

Survival Training

In addition to scuba training, MOL pilots also participated in survival training. Macleay explained, "The survival training was, if you've got to deorbit, you deorbit. And where you come down, you come down, and you'd better be able to hang on for a while until somebody can come get you."[80] According to Abrahamson, "One of the things we did was we had jungle survival, desert survival, water survival, all of these survival tests. And they weren't just tests, they were schools."[81] Macleay was the first to go to training and recalled, "I was the guy on the flight crew that did most of the survival stuff. I was the guinea pig. Because we were going to land in the water, everybody said, 'Well everybody needs to go to water survival. So Macleay, you take a doctor, Elliot Thresher, and you guys go down and go through water survival school at Homestead [in Florida].' So I went down and went through water survival school and thought, 'That's a lot of fun!' I came back and said, 'Everybody needs to go!' So I got to go again. Then after that, we decided, 'Well, you really ought to go through and be in a pressure suit, not just a regular suit.' So we all went again."[82]

Of water survival school, Abrahamson recalled, "I remember in the water survival training program, they brought you up on this parachute kite, and we were in pressure suits, which we didn't like. Then they cut you loose, and you go floating down. You go out and you get your gear, your little boat, your little thing, you get that deployed, and then you get up in it. Then you find that they have punched a hole in every one of them. So you get in, and it's hard to get in, in your pressure suit. So once you're in there, you're looking around and, good! You're in the bay outside, away from Homestead in the big bay there. There are sharks around, but you didn't see them. So you're in now, and you're feeling really good. Then you look down, 'Wait a minute.' You see bubbles coming out of your rubber raft. They had taught you how to put a little clamp in there that stops it. So you go, 'Damn.' You crawl in the water again, get the system out, make it, fix it, then crawl out again. 'Phew, I got that one. Now what?' It was great fun."[83]

Several MOL pilots returned to water survival training later in their careers. After transferring to NASA, Truly recalled one harrowing experience during water survival training at Homestead in which, he recalled, "I damn near got killed."[84] For one particular training exercise, crew members were in a full pressure suit, dropped on a raft, and expected to practice repairing the raft. After successfully completing the exercise, crew members jumped in the water and were to be picked up by boat from there. In Truly's case, the rubber neck dam on his helmet was not completely zipped up, affecting the pressure of the suit and preventing the air valve from correctly dispensing the exhaled carbon dioxide. With a malfunctioning valve, Truly explained, "You began to suffocate. And that's happened to me. It didn't happen until the very end because we stayed at the raft for about an hour, then we lowered the visor and hopped in the water. We were to be there and then the boat would come pick us up. As soon as I lowered the visor, I mean within 1 ½ or 2 minutes, I was suffocating. On top of that, the damn visor mechanism malfunctioned and I couldn't raise the visor. I was trapped. I remember thinking, 'This is how it is to die.' It was a beautiful day, and I waved at the guys on the boat, which were not very far away, and they thought I was just waving at them. Finally they realized something was wrong. They came over, and just about the time they got to me, I gave it all the strength that I could, and I did raise the visor. When I raised the visor, of course, I took a big gulp of air, and I was fine." Reflecting on the danger of training exercises for both the MOL program and NASA, Truly explained, "That's one of the interesting things about the space program, that you do so many different kinds of training, either airplanes or survival or parachuting or whatever. And any one of them, you do it wrong, it can get you."[85]

The pilots also participated in jungle survival school. Abrahamson explained, "For jungle survival, all of us went down to Panama and that was fun."[86] Truly hoped to make a trip of it, recalling, "Jack Finley and I wanted to ride a cruise ship down there, but they wouldn't let us because it would take too long. So we flew down there through Central America on a Gooney Bird, a DC-3."[87] Macleay recalled, "After a few days of classes, they dropped us off in a helicopter out in the middle of the jungle. We had a Panamanian guide named Tuli Rosa. He was supposed to keep us out of trouble."[88]

Survival school was about learning to survive in and off the jungle. Truly recalled, "We lived in the jungle for, I don't remember, maybe out there a week or several days. We built a structure that we called the O-Club [Officer's Club] and we would live off the wildlife in the jungle."[89] Macleay remembered, "Dick Lawyer, who we'd call the great white hunter, had one survival rifle that was an over-and-under. It had a .22 on bottom and I think a .410 shotgun on the top. I think that's what it was. We're hiking down the trail, single-file through the jungle, and Tuli's slashing with his machete, making a path. All of a sudden, he holds up his hand and he takes the rifle away from Dick and he goes, 'Pow!' and he shoots this wild turkey. Man, we had food right off the bat! We had a wild turkey… Then Dick went out hunting and brought back two macaws that he shot. They didn't taste that good. But we learned how to get palm hearts, cut down a whole damn palm tree to get a palm heart. But the jungle was full of them."[90]

For the crew, survival school was about learning vital skills and also enjoying training with friends. Macleay remembered, "We had built what we called the officer's club… It had a fire pit and little shed over a bench we could sit on. We built all that there. We had our fire going one night and a bat flew through, and Hank Hartsfield jumped right in my lap; it scared the hell out of him. In the meantime, there were all these guides trying to catch you, all the natives. You had a hat, and if they got your hat, they could turn the hat in for $5 or something. So they were looking for you."[91] As part of the training, it was essential that the crew learn how to get rescued. Macleay explained, "We were supposed to get spotted. I remember we had parachute cord, we had a couple flares, and we had to learn how to throw the flare up high into this tree because you're in the jungle and you had to throw it up high into the tree on the string so it would stay up there lit so somebody could find you. We called it the old 'flare in the tree trick.'"[92]

Survival school did not lack for excitement. Macleay recalled, "Coming out, we had to get in the Chagres River and float downstream. We're all floating down the river, just having a great time in our little life vests, using it as kind of an inner tube. We got all strung out, we were really strung out. Of course you want to be on the outside of the turn because it's faster, so everybody would be saying, 'Left! Left! Right! Right!' And you'd be paddling to get on the right side… The river was coming up fast. It turned out we were in a flash flood and we didn't know it. The river went up about 12 feet in about 30 minutes and we were in the middle of it. I'll never forget… I'm kind of in the back and we hear from the guys ahead, 'Left, left!' And then I hear Tuli saying, 'No, no! Right, right!' There was a huge boulder that became a waterfall and we all went over the top of it and, man, I wasn't sure I was coming up. I must have gone down, up and down about four or five times, this huge eddy. We all made it out of there without getting hurt, but man, at the end of it, when I finally got out, and I'm a pretty good swimmer, I went over to the bank and just sat there for a little bit because I was scared. Then the rest of it was…. It was something else. That was our jungle survival. It was kind of fun."[93] Bobko recalled thinking, "I don't think this is survival practice anymore."[94]

Cross-Organizational Training

A few crew members were able to participate in NASA training as well. Truly recalled, "The program was a NASA program and Martin [in] Baltimore got the contract. It was to send a series of three-manned crews up there and live in a simulated Apollo simulator for a week, which was the approximate duration of the Apollo mission. Many test pilots from Edwards, NASA astronauts, and eventually some MOL astronauts went up there and participated in the program. It was a lot of fun. We worked hard training for the seven-day simulation. The crew that I was on was Jimmy Taylor and Greg Neubeck and me. We spent about six weeks, if I remember right, up in Baltimore."[95]

As a bonus, while there, they trained with some local celebrities. Truly recalled, "They had a contract with a good friend named Eddie Block who was head trainer for the Baltimore Colts. We went up there in June or July, when the Colts were out of season. Eddie had a contract to come over and give us physical training. We would work all day and then go work out with Eddie for a couple or three hours and then go to the bar, go have dinner, and get up early the next morning and do it again… A lot of the Colts players lived in Baltimore and so they would come over, since Eddie was their trainer. We had a nice gym that had handball courts, they would come over and we would work out and play handball with them. I got to play handball with John Unitas and Alan Ameche and a whole bunch of the Colts from that era. They were a lot bigger than we were, but we hit it off real well."[96]

Some of the training was also academic. During July 1967, the MOL program office coordinated training for crew members with the National Photographic Interpretation Center (NPIC) in Washington, DC.[97] The two-day indoctrination program was designed "to introduce the astronauts to the general subject of photographic intelligence and to provide them with an initial background in target recognition prior to their participation as subjects in Active Target Indicator Mode Simulation."[98] The entire second group of crew members and several of the first participated in the 1967 training. The MOL office continued to coordinate with NPIC, and Herres, Peterson, and Abrahamson all participated in a two-week orientation training at NPIC facilities in July 1968.[99] The MOL system was unique in its design to utilize man to help select active and significant reconnaissance targets, and the NPIC training was essential in training man to be effective in this role.

MOL's Secrecy

Due to the nature of MOL, portions of the program had to be conducted in the open. Program officials understood, "In all probability, a modest public information release will be associated with at least the initial fully manned MOL launches."[100] But MOL was a highly classified program and information was closely guarded. One policy document from 1966 stated, "The Department of Defense MOL is not a cover or clandestine overflight program, although the primary mission is covert."[101]

One of the major concerns about publicity was the impact acknowledging the reconnaissance mission of MOL would have on international relations. In 1965, many were hopeful that the Cold War tensions between the U.S. and U.S.S.R. were beginning to thaw and progress toward disarmament would continue. Despite tensions on the ground, space had remained peaceful and unarmed. Some feared that releasing information about MOL would diminish the "peaceful space" image of the U.S. internationally. The month following the announcement of MOL, news articles highlighted a public hesitation about space reconnaissance and noted that the announcement had caused some "disquiet."[102] By October 1965, a Soviet Foreign Ministry Officer, G.S. Stashevski, conveyed to U.S. representatives "the serious apprehension of the Soviet scientific community" regarding the MOL program.[103] The concern about MOL was significant enough that U.S.S.R. representatives were raising the issue in bilateral talks. However, the Soviets used MOL as more of a political tool and did not seem to fear it; in fact, they "reiterated their intention to launch one of their own."[104] One research memorandum explained, "Moscow seems to be more acutely concerned with the ins and outs of political exploitation of the U.S. announcement than with the long-anticipated U.S. MOL Program as a potential strategic threat."[105]

In addition to the general concerns about national security, officials limited public information about the program for fear MOL would be misrepresented. In late October 1965, Assistant Secretary of Defense for Public Affairs Arthur Sylvester issued a DoD policy for handling MOL public statements which specified that all national-level press queries were to be referred to his office for response.[106] Additionally, all speeches and interviews regarding MOL were discouraged and had to be cleared through the Assistant Secretary of Defense for Public Affairs' office.[107] The official Public Affairs guidance stated that the objectives were "to localize and minimize publicity on the MOL program. Information proposed for release should be limited to that data which would probably become public because of unavoidable public visibility. Such information will be released in a modest, low-key manner designed to avoid widespread adverse reactions on the part of the news media which would tend to overemphasize the military as opposed to scientific objectives of the program."[108] In line with the emphasis on the scientific opportunities available with MOL, in an October 1965 decision, the MOL Policy Committee agreed that MOL crew members would be designated as "MOL Aerospace Research Pilots."[109]

Program secrecy also visibly impacted MOL contractors. Albert Crews visited Rochester once and recalled, "I was impressed by the operation there."[110] Due to security concerns in the MOL program, DNRO Flax emphasized, "It is essential that neither the contractor [Eastman Kodak] nor these particular facilities [in Rochester] be identified with the MOL program, nor do we wish to highlight even an unidentified DoD program of large magnitude optics of this size."[111] Since the Air Force contract with Eastman Kodak was classified and the public was unaware of what they were building at Rochester, Crews explained, "They [Eastman Kodak] dug deep down in the ground because if we had a laboratory with a mirror in it and it was 30 feet, the laboratory was 30 feet long and it needed something 30 feet high where you could look at things. They dug a big hole in the ground so the building wouldn't stick up so high. It seemed like the other side wouldn't have guessed that we had a mirror as big as we had if there was no building anywhere of that size."[112]

> *"It was hard to talk about anything, just about everything was covered under the secrecy..."*

For the selected crew members, program security also had a very personal impact. Strict classification meant that crew members' families had a very limited idea of the program and often could not know where crew members were working. Crippen recalled, "We'd go visit places like Eastman Kodak, and we couldn't say where we were going or when we'd be back."[113] Crews stated that he told his family, "I was on the program, but I didn't tell them what I was going to do. We were going to ride up in the Gemini and work in the lab for 30 days and then come home. We were going to run experiments."[114] Bobko explained, "It was hard to talk about anything, just about everything was covered under the secrecy of 'It's the MOL program,' and that's about when everybody shut up."[115]

According to MOL policy, limited information was released publicly about each of the crew members, after which their public exposure was limited and controlled. Crew members were forbidden from giving interviews. Crew members were "required at all times to maintain a high standard for moral, ethical, and military conduct."[116] As part of the program plan, crew members were to return to earth in the Gemini capsule carrying "a substantial portion of the mission photographic product on-board."[117] In case of emergency landing, crew members were instructed to exercise U.S. sovereignty over all equipment and to refrain from providing information on the program or reconnaissance information collected to anyone during either incarceration or interrogation.[118] Secrecy was so ingrained in those involved in the program that 35 years after MOL was canceled, when asked about the reconnaissance mission, Bobko explained, "I'm still a little edgy about talking about it because nobody's ever talked about it."[119]

MOL's Relationship with NASA

President Eisenhower established the National Aeronautics and Space Administration in 1958 as the United States' civilian organization for space exploration. By the mid-1960s when MOL was getting off the ground, NASA's projects Mercury, Gemini, and Apollo were all underway. Additionally, NASA was exploring opportunities for a space station and initiated the Skylab program in 1965. Space exploration was in its infancy; both NASA and the military were staking their claims, creating a tenuous balance between cooperation and competition.

Over the life of the program, NASA and MOL leadership struggled to maintain a cooperative relationship. In early 1964, a Space Systems Division study, against the wishes of NASA, recommended that the Air Force contract directly with McDonnell Aircraft Corporation for MOL's Gemini B.[120] Frustrated, NASA requested that MOL compromise and contract for the Gemini B through NASA instead. This was only one contract among a myriad of issues. Later that year, Secretary of Defense McNamara suggested several compromises to NASA Administrator James Webb, arguing, "This appears the best approach if the MOL is viewed (as I view it) as a necessary precursor to an operational space station should it later be determined that such is required."[121] In order to avoid duplicative efforts, McNamara suggested both agencies accept MOL as the forerunner to a NASA space station. As such, NASA should accept management responsibility of the scientific program to be carried out using MOL, while the Air Force continues as operating manager of the program. McNamara suggested the program be coordinated through a joint DoD/NASA board and, after successful flight, further decisions could be made regarding the future necessity of a military or scientific space station and who would be in charge.[122]

James E. Webb.
Source: CSNR Reference Collection.

Much of the NASA/DoD frustration remained at the management and leadership levels. Bobko recalled observing a relationship that was not always harmonious, but stated, "I was never up high enough to see how that was being done. But I know that there were clashes between them."[123] To promote cooperation, in 1966 the MOL office opened a position within the MOL Systems Office to NASA employees, requesting that NASA identify potential applicants.[124] NASA continued to have a presence in the MOL program office for the life of the program.

In addition to competition over resources and priority, MOL security concerns proved a nearly insurmountable barrier to developing a cooperative relationship with NASA. Truly summarized, "NASA worked as hard to get publicity as the NRO did to avoid publicity."[125] Reflecting on the relationship, Abrahamson commented, "In MOL, we should have been much closer to NASA, but we felt like we couldn't because of the classification of the program. We saw them, they knew we existed, and we'd try to get to know each other and listen. But we couldn't talk about it very much. So in that sense, it was hard."[126] But security concerns did not completely prohibit collaboration. In 1968, Maj. Gen. Stewart informed DNRO Flax, "I have assured him [Charles W. Mathews – NASA Deputy Associate Administrator] that NASA is welcome to any and all information on MOL (he recognized that NASA must accept appropriate security classifications), that we would be willing to study in reasonable depth any NASA questions not pertinent to the present MOL Program, etc."[127] Within weeks, MOL leadership scheduled a meeting with NASA to discuss any potential capability offered NASA by MOL program hardware, although some level of cooperation regarding shared hardware had been ongoing for some time.[128] That autumn, two MOL flight surgeons were assigned to each manned Apollo mission through all stages of pre-launch preparation and mission operations. The arrangement was mutually beneficial as NASA gained needed bioastronautics support, while MOL's flight surgeons received the benefit of both training and experience in manned spaceflight operations.[129]

On the working level, however, many MOL crew members saw little interaction with NASA. Crews recalled, "I don't think there was any relationship at all between NASA and the MOL program."[130] According to him, NASA "wasn't a lot different than the way we operated in the Air Force, except it seemed like they had more money and more equipment and more support."[131] Bobko recalled several former NASA employees who worked on the MOL program, stating, "They brought some of their knowledge into the MOL program."[132] Although the NASA/MOL relationship was fragile, the crew members were generally unaffected.

The MOL Build-Up

In June 1966, General Schriever announced that the definition phase of MOL had been completed, and "the program as now defined and recommended for funding approval will satisfy the national need for high resolution satellite reconnaissance photography..."[133] By the end of the summer, Air Force Systems Command, NASA, the Department of Defense Manager for Manned Space Flight Support Operations, the Department of the Army, the Department of the Navy, the U.S. Air Force Headquarters, Strategic Air Command, and Military Airlift Command were agreed upon support of MOL.[134] In January 1967, DNRO Flax authorized MOL to proceed with the engineering development phase of the program, releasing $120 million in funds for FY 1967.[135] Shortly thereafter, the DoD awarded Santa Fe and Stolte of Lancaster, California the contract to build the MOL launch complex at Vandenberg Air Force Base, a facility eventually known as Space Launch Complex 6 (SLC-6).[136]

In addition to attaining a budget and support, MOL management continued to outline clear, streamlined objectives. In February 1967, flight objectives for the MOL program were released which specified both general test objectives of MOL's flight test phase, divided into three tiers, and an orderly approach for achieving those defined objectives.[137] The mandatory objectives included demonstrating MOL's ability to acquire photographs of high intelligence value, obtaining quantitative data on the nature and value of man's critical contributions, and demonstrating the 30-day capability of the program. Leadership defined the secondary objectives, as long as they did not interfere with the program's primary objectives, as obtaining data to assess military worth of other possible missions in space, obtaining data regarding the optical technology and design to lead to ground resolution approaching the atmospheric limit, and collecting bioastronautics data. Included as a tertiary objective, MOL astronauts were to conduct experiments to contribute to the improvement of military space technology and experiments of a scientific nature.[138]

After years of planning and negotiating, the program achieved a steady development pace in 1968. Abrahamson recalled that 1968 was "the first year that was really a big budget year."[139] The program office had overcome many of the initial hurdles, and program leadership looked forward optimistically. Many were hopeful about the future of MOL. The seven-launch program, defined as Block I, was only the beginning. Upon completion of Block I, the proposed Block II consisted of three or four systems, both manned and unmanned. The Block II systems would incorporate modest changes to increase flexibility, maximize quality, and to extend the manned mission from 30 days to 40.[140] The proposal for MOL's Block III systems allowed for a variety of concepts, but it hoped for 50-60 day manned missions and 70-90 day unmanned missions.[141] A number of studies were completed to evaluate MOL's potential contributions, finding that MOL could provide photography at sufficient resolution for technical intelligence on space targets and could make significant contributions to the policing of arms limitation agreements. One study also found, "MOL has some potential to obtain coverage of targets or areas during periods of international tension and crisis. During the Cuban missile crisis, the value of VHR photography to provide easily understood and incontrovertible evidence for national decision making was clearly demonstrated. MOL will be on orbit about 25 per cent of the time during the year and can pass daily over a point of interest with little penalty."[142] Although many saw great potential for MOL, it faced a number of challenges as well – challenges which ultimately led to its demise.

Endnotes

1. Agenda and highlights, Sub: Air Force MOL Policy Committee Meeting, 14 October 1965, Job 199700097-08-030-3, NROARC.
2. Ibid.
3. Oral History Interview with Karol Bobko, 3 April 2014, p. 5, CSNR/RC.
4. Ibid, p. 6.
5. Oral History Interview with Robert Crippen, 24 March 2014, p. 4, CSNR/RC.
6. Memorandum, Louis F. Mazza (NRO Staff Chief Security Officer) to Reber, Sub: MOL-USIB Relationship, 21 December 1965, Job 199700083-13-002G, NROARC.
7. Oral History Interview with Lachlan Macleay, 2 June 2014, p. 7, CSNR/RC.
8. Ibid, p. 12.
9. Oral History Interview with Richard Truly, 4 June 2014, p. 7, CSNR/RC.
10. Oral History Interview with James Abrahamson, 20 June 2013, p. 5, CSNR/RC.
11. Oral History Interview with Albert Crews, 24 March 2014, p. 6, CSNR/RC.
12. Oral History Interview with Robert Crippen, 24 March 2014, p. 5, CSNR/RC.
13. Oral History Interview, Karol Bobko, 3 April 2014, p. 13, CSNR/RC.
14. Oral History Interview with Lachlan Macleay, 2 June 2014, p. 10, CSNR/RC.
15. Memorandum for Record, Stewart, Sub: PRC Meeting 6 May 1968, 14 May 1968, Job 199700066-05-008, NROARC.
16. Oral History Interview with Robert Crippen, 24 March 2014, p. 5, CSNR/RC.
17. Ibid, p. 7.
18. Oral History Interview with Albert Crews, 24 March 2014, p. 6, CSNR/RC.
19. Ibid.
20. Ibid.
21. Oral History Interview with Robert Crippen, 24 March 2014, p. 6, CSNR/RC.
22. Oral History Interview with Albert Crews, 24 March 2014, p. 5, CSNR/RC.
23. Oral History Interview with Karol Bobko, 3 April 2014, p. 6, CSNR/RC.
24. Ibid, p. 13.
25. Ibid, p. 6.
26. Oral History Interview with Richard Truly, 4 June 2014, p. 7, CSNR/RC.
27. Oral History Interview with Albert Crews, 24 March 2014, p. 7, CSNR/RC.
28. Oral History Interview with Karol Bobko, 3 April 2014, p. 21, CSNR/RC.
29. Oral History Interview with Richard Truly, 4 June 2014, p. 6, CSNR/RC.
30. Oral History Interview with Lachlan Macleay, 2 June 2014, p. 8, CSNR/RC.
31. Oral History Interview with Richard Truly, 4 June 2014, p. 8, CSNR/RC.
32. Oral History Interview with Karol Bobko, 3 April 2014, p. 22, CSNR/RC.
33. Oral History Interview with Richard Truly, 4 June 2014, p. 7, CSNR/RC.
34. An Operations Concept for MOL/Dorian Manned/Automatic Configuration, 15 June 1967, Job 199700070-02-024-036, NROARC.

35 Oral History Interview with Lachlan Macleay, 2 June 2014, p. 8, CSNR/RC.

36 Oral History Interview with Karol Bobko, 3 April 2014, p. 25, CSNR/RC.

37 Memorandum, Stewart and Ferguson to Secretary of the Air Force, Sub: MOL Monthly Status Report for June, 6 July 1967, Job 199700033-08-028A, NROARC.

38 Oral History Interview with Lachlan Macleay, 2 June 2014, p. 9, CSNR/RC.

39 Oral History Interview with Richard Truly, 4 June 2014, p. 7, CSNR/RC.

40 An Operations Concept for MOL/Dorian Manned/Automatic Configuration, 15 June 1967, Job 199700070-02-024-036, NROARC.

41 Oral History Interview with Richard Truly, 4 June 2014, p. 7, CSNR/RC.

42 Oral History Interview with James Abrahamson, 20 June 2013, p. 5, CSNR/RC.

43 Oral History Interview with Karol Bobko, 3 April 2014, p. 25, CSNR/RC.

44 Oral History Interview with Richard Truly, 4 June 2014, p. 8, CSNR/RC.

45 Oral History Interview with James Abrahamson, 20 June 2013, p. 6, CSNR/RC.

46 Briefing Charts, Sub: Review of Program Status and Problems for Vice Director MOL, 7 July 1967, Job 199700066-05-012-003, NROARC.

47 Ibid.

48 An Operations Concept for MOL/Dorian Manned/Automatic Configuration, 15 June 1967, Job 199700070-02-024-036, NROARC.

49 Oral History Interview with Karol Bobko, 2 April 2014, p. 12, CSNR/RC.

50 Briefing Charts, Sub: Review of Program Status and Problems for Vice Director MOL, 7 July 1967, Job 199700066-05-012-003, NROARC.

51 Letter, Stewart to Flax, Sub: MOL/DORIAN Reconnaissance System briefing, 23 September 1966, Job 199700063-04-016-023, NROARC.

52 Ibid.

53 Memorandum, H. Bernstein to Bleymaier, Sub: Viewer Requirements: Associated Crew Tasks and Capabilities, 17 December 1968, Job 199900021-02-050, NROARC.

54 The Roles of Man in MOL – Volume I, Manned Orbiting Laboratory Program Office, 1 June 1969, Job 199700042-04-009, NROARC.

55 Ibid.

56 Ibid.

57 Ibid.

58 Ibid.

59 Ibid.

60 Oral History Interview with Robert Crippen, 24 March 2014, p. 5, CSNR/RC.

61 Manned Orbiting Laboratory Program Plan Volume 1 of 2, undated, Job 199700066-05-014, NROARC.

62 Ibid.

63 Ibid.

64 Ibid.

65 Ibid.

66 Ibid.

67   Ibid.

68   Ibid.

69   Oral History Interview with Richard Truly, 4 June 2014, p. 8, CSNR/RC.

70   Oral History Interview with Karol Bobko, 3 April 2014, p. 8, CSNR/RC.

71   Ibid, p. 11.

72   Oral History Interview with Lachlan Macleay, 2 June 2014, p. 11, CSNR/RC.

73   Oral History Interview with James Abrahamson, 18 July 2013, p. 7, CSNR/RC.

74   Ibid.

75   Oral History Interview with Lachlan Macleay, 2 June 2014, p. 14, CSNR/RC.

76   Oral History Interview with James Abrahamson, 18 July 2013, p. 7, CSNR/RC.

77   Oral History Interview with Lachlan Macleay, 2 June 2014, p. 14, CSNR/RC.

78   Oral History Interview with Albert Crews, 24 March 2014, p. 6, CSNR/RC.

79   Monthly Management Report for 25 April – 25 May 1968, Bleymaier, 17 June 1968, Job 199700033-09-014-006, NROARC.

80   Oral History Interview with Lachlan Macleay, 2 June 2014, p. 15, CSNR/RC.

81   Oral History Interview with James Abrahamson, 18 July 2013, p. 13, CSNR/RC.

82   Oral History Interview with Lachlan Macleay, 2 June 2014, p. 10, CSNR/RC.

83   Oral History Interview with James Abrahamson, 18 July 2013, p. 14, CSNR/RC.

84   Oral History Interview with Richard Truly, 11 June 2014, p. 12, CSNR/RC.

85   Ibid, p. 12.

86   Ibid, p. 13.

87   Oral History Interview with Richard Truly, 11 June 2014, p. 11, CSNR/RC.

88   Oral History Interview with Lachlan Macleay, 2 June 2014, p. 10, CSNR/RC.

89   Oral History Interview with Richard Truly, 11 June 2014, p. 11, CSNR/RC.

90   Oral History Interview with Lachlan Macleay, 2 June 2014, p. 10, CSNR/RC.

91   Ibid, p. 11.

92   Ibid.

93   Ibid.

94   Panel Discussion with Karol Bobko, MOL Declassification Event at Dayton, Ohio, 22 October 2015.

95   Oral History Interview with Richard Truly, 4 June 2014, p. 11, CSNR/RC.

96   Ibid.

97   Memorandum, Sub: NPIC support for the DORIAN Program, 13 January 1967, Job 199700070-02-024-027, NROARC.

98   Memorandum, Stewart and Ferguson to Secretary of the Air Force, Sub: MOL Monthly Status Report for March, 5 April 1967, Job 199700033-08-027F, NROARC.

99   Memorandum, Stewart to Flax, Sub: NPIC training for astronauts, 5 July 1968, Job 199700083-12-009, NROARC.

100 Policy Relating to Manned Orbiting Laboratory (MOL) Astronauts, 23 December 1966, Job 199700050-02-008-015, NROARC; Memorandum, Flax to Director MOL, Sub: Policy Relating to MOL Astronauts, 28 December 1966, Job 199700050-02-008-015, NROARC.

101 Policy Relating to Manned Orbiting Laboratory (MOL) Astronauts, 23 December 1966, attached to Memorandum for the Director, MOL, Flax, Sub: Policy Relating to MOL Astronauts, 28 December 1966, Job 199700050-02-008-015, NROARC.

102 Impact of Recent Publicity on MOL Program, Job 200200001-07-008, NROARC.

103 Memorandum, USUN (Goldberg) to Department of Space, Sub: Outer Space, MOL, 11 October 1965, Job 199700042-04-015-011, NROARC.

104 Research Memorandum, INR Thomas L. Hughes, Sub: Soviet Criticism of the US MOL Program, 19 October 1965, Job 199700042-04-015-014, NROARC.

105 Ibid.

106 Memorandum, Schriever to Secretary of the Air Force, Sub: MOL Monthly Status Report for October 1965, 8 November 1965, Job 199700033-08-024-002, NROARC.

107 Ibid.

108 Public Affairs Guidance – DoD MOL Program, undated, Job 199700033-09-017-012, NROARC.

109 Memorandum for Secretariat Record, signed by Evans, Sub: Proceedings of Air Force MOL Policy Committee Meeting 65-3, 14 October 1965, Job 199700033-09-016-003, NROARC.

110 Oral History Interview with Albert Crews, 24 March 2014, p. 10, CSNR/RC.

111 Memorandum, Flax to the Director of Defense Research & Engineering, Sub: Eastman Kodak Corporation Facilities for MOL, 4 April 1966, Job 199700050-02-005-015, NROARC.

112 Oral History Interview with Albert Crews, 24 March 2014, p. 10, CSNR/RC.

113 Oral History Interview with Robert Crippen, 24 March 2014, p. 9, CSNR/RC.

114 Oral History Interview with Albert Crews, 24 March 2014, p. 9, CSNR/RC.

115 Oral History Interview with Karol Bobko, 3 April 2014, p. 7, CSNR/RC.

116 Policy Relating to Manned Orbiting Laboratory (MOL) Astronauts, 23 December 1966, attached to Memorandum for the Director, MOL, Flax, Sub: Policy Relating to MOL Astronauts, 28 December 1966, Job 199700050-02-008-015, NROARC.

117 Ibid.

118 Ibid.

119 Oral History Interview with Karol Bobko, 3 April 2014, p. 7, CSNR/RC.

120 Memorandum, Flax to Director Research & Engineering, Sub: MOL, 19 January 1964, Job 199700050-02-002-025, NROARC.

121 Letter, McNamara to Webb (NASA Administrator), 25 September 1964, Job 199700050-02-002-042, NROARC.

122 Ibid.

123 Oral History Interview with Karol Bobko, 3 April 2014, p. 14, CSNR/RC.

124 Memorandum, Evans to Secretary of the Air Force, Sub: MOL Monthly Status Report for August, 7 September 1966, Job 199700033-08-025D, NROARC.

125 Panel Discussion with Richard Truly, MOL Declassification Event at Dayton, Ohio, 22 October 2015.

126 Oral History Interview with James Abrahamson, 20 June 2013, p. 21-22, CSNR/RC.

127 Memorandum, Stewart to Flax, Sub: NASA Interest in MOL, 20 June 1968, Job 199700046-03-012-006, NROARC.

128 Memorandum, Stewart and Ferguson to Secretary of the Air Force, Sub: MOL Monthly Status Report for June, 3 July 1968, Job 199700033-08-029F, NROARC; Memorandum, Evans to Flax, Sub: Astronomical Mission for MOL, 7 February 1967, Job 199700050-02-009-011, NROARC.

129 Memorandum for Record, Stewart, Sub: Program Review Council Meeting 24 October 1968, 2 November 1968, Job 199700066-05-019C, NROARC.

130 Oral History Interview with Albert Crews, 24 March 2014, p. 9, CSNR/RC.

131 Ibid.

132 Oral History Interview with Karol Bobko, 3 April 2014, p. 14, CSNR/RC.

133 Memorandum, Schriever to Secretary of the Air Force, Sub: MOL Program Plan and Funding Requirements, 22 June 1966, Job 199700050-02-005-022, NROARC.

134 Headquarters Air Force Systems Command Operation Order for the support of the MOL Program, 4 August 1966, Job 199700050-02-006-006, NROARC.

135 Memorandum, Flax to Director MOL, Sub: Authorization to Proceed with the Engineering Development Phase of the MOL Program, 13 January 1967, Job 199700076-02-007-001, NROARC.

136 Memorandum, Evans and Ferguson to Secretary of the Air Force, Sub: MOL Monthly Status Report for January, 7 February 1967, Job 199700033-08-027D, NROARC.

137 MOL Program directive No. 67-2, Sub: Flight Objectives for the MOL Program, 8 February 1967, Job 199700050-02-009-012, NROARC.

138 Ibid.

139 Oral History Interview with James Abrahamson, 20 June 2013, p. 10, CSNR/RC.

140 Statement of Work, undated, Job 199700063-04-018-003, NROARC.

141 Ibid.

142 The Need for Very High Resolution Imagery and its Contribution to DOD Operations and Decisions Volume I – Executive Summary, November 1968, Job 199700057-05-001, NROARC.

Chapter 4

THE END OF MOL

Although MOL crew members had been selected and engineering and development work was well underway, MOL faced intense scrutiny and criticism on a number of fronts. Many critics questioned whether or not MOL should be a manned program. Others felt the potential risk of damaging international relations was too high, MOL's contribution to national intelligence of VHR photography was not sufficient justification for such a costly program, the program overlapped too much with NASA's Apollo program, and MOL had grown too expensive and fallen too far behind schedule. Facing major budget issues and inadequate support, MOL's critics eventually succeeded, and the program was canceled before it ever had a chance to prove its worth.

The Debate over the Necessity of Man

Putting man in space in the 1960s was dangerous and expensive. Over the life of the entire MOL program, the debate raged over what man could contribute to the program and whether or not it was worth the risk and money. One solution to this debate was to concurrently develop both manned and unmanned capabilities for MOL, a recommendation the President's Science Advisor, Dr. Donald Hornig, made as early as 1965.[1] Dr. Hornig chaired the President's Scientific Advisory Committee (PSAC) while Dr. Edwin H. Land, a scientist and inventor who founded the Polaroid Company, chaired

Edwin H. Land. Source: CSNR Reference Collection.

the PSAC Reconnaissance Panel. The Reconnaissance Panel as a whole adhered to the solution of concurrent development. Dr. Edward Purcell, longtime presidential science advisor and member of the PSAC Reconnaissance Panel, argued that including automatic features in the MOL camera system would also improve the manned system.[2]

Dr. Hornig and Secretary of the Air Force Harold Brown reached an agreement on 23 August 1965.[3] According to their agreement, realizing the desired superior resolution was a high priority national goal achievable in both the manned and unmanned systems. All conversion equipment required for the unmanned system would be developed concurrently with the manned system, although the manned system would receive both the financial and management priority.[4] Recognizing that the manned system did offer more flexibility, both parties expected that the unmanned system would eventually be flown for routine missions, while the manned system would be saved for situations which required special capabilities.[5] Under the direction of DNRO McMillan, program officials incorporated the PSASC's recommendation into MOL's schedule. Optimistic early plans called for an unmanned system to fly only nine months after the first manned flight.[6]

These design changes were made after serious consideration, and both manned and unmanned options were extensively explored. The DIAMOND II study, comparing the anticipated successful reconnaissance products achieved through the manned and unmanned systems, resulted in a 91-page report.[7] The study found that by using man as a weather scout, "A manned DORIAN system will successfully photograph approximately 18-20 percent more targets than an unmanned system when employed on identical intelligence-collection missions against average Sino-Soviet Bloc climatology."[8] Likewise, studies comparing the two versions of the system and directed by the DNRO in September 1965 concluded that the automatic system was feasible, but it would yield slightly degraded mission resolution.[9] The unmanned system was also heavier, an issue which would need to be addressed in order to fit within the weight restrictions of the launch vehicle. Given these constraints, the unmanned system was not expected to be ready to fly until at least January 1970.[10] Despite the few disadvantages, leadership agreed to pursue the plan for concurrent development, adding two more flights to the initial seven-flight plan.[11]

This compromise was tenuous and did not last long. Only two months later, the Bureau of Budget, in a memorandum to Secretary of Defense Robert McNamara, suggested that the resolution on the unmanned system was potentially just as good as the resolution on the manned MOL and proposed that the Defense Department pursue an unmanned-only system in order to save costs.[12] Instead of dismissing man completely, the PSAC did continue to push for a more automated system. Dr. Donald H. Steininger from the PSAC panel on reconnaissance claimed, "The DoD is 'killing itself' in attempts to justify the man" – a wasted effort.[13] He argued that the panel accepted man as a part of MOL, but still hoped to see much of MOL automated so that man could be free to experiment. In summary, Steininger argued, "The PSAC Panel wants to release man to do his job."[14]

The following year, however, the Reconnaissance Panel expressed disappointment by the lack of imagination in using man in a diagnostic role.[15] Although the PSAC had accepted man as part of MOL, Dr. Steininger argued that, if pressed hard, Dr. Land would probably still maintain that man in MOL was not worth the cost.[16] MOL leadership met with the PSAC Reconnaissance Panel in August 1967 and argued for man's role, stating, "In a gross sense it is possible to separate the areas of the crew's contributions into three categories; namely, their primary role to aid in the realization at the earliest possible date of a mature system (both the manned and unmanned configurations), and their subsidiary roles of enhancing the value of the primary reconnaissance mission and providing, by virtue of their presence aboard manned flights, system capabilities in addition to those associated with the primary reconnaissance mission."[17] The MOL team argued that additional functions offered by man onboard included verification of targets, visual reconnaissance, and the use of special films.[18] After the meeting, MOL leadership documented that Dr. Land was skeptical about the usefulness of man in MOL, though he did respond well to the introduction of the astronaut's Acquisition and Tracking Scope that Macleay and Truly were developing.[19]

Although the PSAC panel claimed to have accepted man, the DoD continued to justify the manned system. A 1966 study titled "Development Problems Inherent in an Unmanned Dorian System" served to reconfirm the validity of the manned approach.[20] Synthesizing data and information from analyses and tests run over the previous year, the study acknowledged that an unmanned system was technically feasible, though it did express concern over the length of time required to bring the unmanned system to maturity. Ultimately, the study found, "The presence of the crew in the initial flights of the MOL system will, by virtue of their abilities to perform switching, maintenance, manual backup, and in particular, diagnostic functions in situations of failure or off-nominal performance, significantly contribute to an early maturing of the unmanned system. At the same time, the missions will simultaneously be gathering high-resolution photography of significant intelligence value."[21] Likewise, DNRO Flax argued that the benefits of man on board MOL included acting as a manual backup for complex automated functions, manual repair or adjustment, greater percentage of cloud-free photography, quick reaction intelligence read-out capability, and target selectivity.[22]

Michael I. Yarymovych.
Source: CSNR Reference Collection.

Acting as a backup for the automatic system, however, was problematic. Albert Crews recalled, "Somewhere along there, it became obvious that all we were was a backup in case the unmanned reconnaissance system didn't work. Because at the time we were selected, the capability, we were told, was a resolution of about five feet on the early vehicles. They wanted [better] resolution. I guess about two years after we were selected, out in L.A., we were invited to the briefings when they had a reconnaissance mission, and they would show the pictures. One time I saw pictures come across there… I told myself, 'I'm probably not going to have a job.' But it was another year or two before they canceled it."[23] Crews was not alone in fearing the automatic system would soon replace the manned. One internal memorandum stated, "There persists within the MOL Program Office the uneasy feeling that man is methodically being eliminated from the MOL Program."[24] As the technology used by the unmanned system improved, the manned system faced increasing skepticism.

Leadership both within and outside of MOL continued to study the issue. In 1967, MOL's technical director, Michael I. Yarymovych, was tasked with comparing the costs of the unmanned and manned systems. However, Yarymovych stated, "These two programs are not directly cost-comparable in terms of timing, risk, quality, and quantity of product, and future potential."[25] Although an unmanned system was estimated at $1.7 to $1.8 billion and the fully manned system was now expected to cost $2.2 billion, Yarymovych emphasized, "The absence of man increases the development risk" and would necessitate more flights.[26] Yarymovych continued, "Nor is it certain that an unmanned system will ever be as reliable as a manned system," while man guaranteed the desired resolution and schedule.[27] Highlighting man's added effectiveness, the faster system development period, and the greater potential for flexibility in flight, Yarymovych concluded, "Thus, in light of all the preceding, it appears conclusive that the additional incremental development cost of developing a manned/unmanned MOL/Dorian system over that of an independent unmanned program is more than offset by both the near term advantages and the long range potential."[28]

> "The absence of man increases the development risk..."

Ultimately, the unmanned system was less certain than the manned system. Fearing the unmanned system would not be ready for flight, causing major delays throughout the program and preventing MOL from accomplishing its program goals, Maj. Gen. Harry Evans proposed making preparations to convert flights 6 and 7 to manned flights, if necessary.[29] Personnel studied the proposal, and MOL engineers discovered that the conversion capability was not currently included but could be with minor changes.[30] By modifying or substituting a limited amount of hardware, the system could be reconfigured to fly either manned or unmanned; that decision would need to be made about six months prior to flight.[31] The MOL Program Office argued that a convertible design was superior, allowing for flexibility based on the current system and international situations.[32]

The issue of man was continually revisited, however, especially as the budget became a more prominent issue. Addressing concerns over the FY 1968 budget, some proposed cutting man either from the first year of MOL flights or replacing him altogether. Although there would be a reduction in cost, the decrease would not be dramatic due to the money already spent on the manned portion of the program.[33] After studying the possibilities, DoD personnel found, "In summary, flying the unmanned MOL configuration first would not reduce FY 1968 costs, would increase total cost, increase technical risks, and probably delay the demonstration of the required operational reconnaissance capability."[34] Going even further, DoD personnel argued that MOL was the most cost-effective solution to the desired capability, stating, "At this point in time, there is real doubt that any program can be constructed that will achieve the required capability – manned or unmanned – more economically than MOL, regardless of when the required capability is desired."[35] Special Projects staff concurred in a 45-page memorandum to the Director of Defense Research and Engineering, stating that the unmanned system was only slightly cheaper, and the advantage of man on board far outweighed the cost.[36]

By early 1968, man was seemingly accepted as an integral part of MOL. Harold Brown stated, "I believe that the present MOL program is a sound undertaking with a high confidence of achieving [superior] resolution and a worthwhile intelligence product on early manned flights."[37] In February 1968, during a MOL briefing to the House Committee on Science and Astronautics, the Committee asked questions about the role of man inflight, man's role in speeding development, and the potential overlap between MOL and NASA programs. Following the briefing, Air Force leadership reported that all of the Committee's questions were answered to their satisfaction.[38] Acknowledging that perhaps one day the system would become fully automatic, at least for the early flights, man was accepted as necessary.

The Soviet Concern

Although many within the U.S. government, especially the Department of Defense, supported MOL, some across the globe did not – particularly the Soviet Union. Cold War tensions and distrust colored the international reception of MOL, and many people feared it was a first step toward armament and weaponry in space.[39] Some at home feared the Russians would exploit MOL for propaganda.[40] To mitigate allegations of armament, the State Department proposed in 1965 that MOL leadership grant Soviet officials permits to inspect the MOL spacecraft for nuclear weapons before all launches.[41] The State Department expected the Soviets to refuse such an offer, but it would demonstrate the U.S.'s credibility and combat allegations that MOL was designed to carry Weapons of Mass Destruction (WMDs).[42]

Secretary of the Air Force Brown immediately and strongly disagreed with the State proposal, arguing that it neglected the potential impact on national security.[43] Dr. Brown stated, "In summary, the State Department draft does not present a convincing argument in favor of a U.S. initiative. I recommend that the Department of Defense maintain a strong opposition to satellite pre-launching inspection at this time."[44] In the weeks that followed, others supported Brown's rejection of the proposal. Deputy Assistant Secretary of Defense Alvin Friedman argued there was little need to even consider a pre-launch inspection program.[45] The Department of Defense argued that the likelihood of a controversy with the Soviets was minimal, and a pre-launch inspection program would only scratch the surface of potential issues with a program like MOL.[46]

In 1966, with a meeting of the Eighteen Nation Disarmament Committee (ENDC) approaching, some officials again raised concerns over MOL and how it would be viewed and used by the international community. Although the Soviets did not initially respond poorly to MOL, it was used as propaganda to sustain criticism that the U.S. was intending to militarize space. In response to these concerns, officials prepared a contingency paper stating, "While many nations have recognized the significant potential offered by this project in the further peaceful exploration of space, we regret that the Soviet Union has taken a view to the contrary, alleging that it is just another manifestation of a U.S. intention to use outer space for other than peaceful purposes."[47] Officials stated that MOL was completely in line with the resolution adopted by the General Assembly of the United Nations on 17 October 1963 which expressed that the exploration and use of outer space should be used only for the betterment of mankind.[48] Reiterating its adherence to policy, the contingency paper stated, "The MOL will be non-aggressive in nature and will be designed to contribute to the further development of technology and equipment essential to manned and unmanned space flights and friendly cooperation among all states in the peaceful exploration of space."[49]

International concern continued to affect public information and treatment of MOL. By mid-1968, some officials hoped to release a few MOL technical papers to scientific and technical society meetings. However, Assistant Secretary of Defense Paul Goulder articulated, "State feels the MOL is a potential inflammable propaganda issue in various UN forums."[50] Although the United States Information Agency (USIA) expected "MOL to be more of a liability than an asset as far as the U.S. overseas information program is concerned," they "did not object to the highly selective" documents to be released.[51] For scientific advancement, some information related to MOL was released, though the nature of the program and reconnaissance mission remained highly classified and tightly guarded.

The Importance of Very High Resolution Reconnaissance

Another debate plaguing MOL concerned the necessity of Very High Resolution reconnaissance photography for national security. High resolution photography was considered excellent, while very high resolution was limited to the superior range – a capability that was debated early in the program.[52] As part of a briefing on MOL, program leadership explained, "It will be remembered that early in the MOL planning stages some experienced contractors expressed considerable doubt that an optical system of the desired performance could be built. Such doubts no longer exist."[53] MOL was expected to deliver the better resolution, and could possibly improve over time.

Although MOL could deliver the high resolution products, some questioned whether or not those products were needed. In a MOL program document, the Associate Group Director within the Operations Directorate of MOL, Harry Bernstein, argued, "The United States has a vital need for intelligence information pertaining to activities/developments within the Sino-Soviet [sic] and other denied areas. For various intelligence purposes, the types, quality, and quantity of information to be collected vary considerably, and therefore, a multiplicity of programs are contributing toward the fulfillment of the overall objective. Of significant importance to the total intelligence picture is the need for very high-resolution photographic coverage primarily for technical intelligence purposes, and it is to this purpose that the MOL/DORIAN Program is oriented."[54] Program leadership argued that there was a clear and definable need for VHR photography, and MOL was going to fill that need.

Critics, however, argued that the high resolution photography available through the KH-8 system was adequate, and the MOL system was far too expensive. These critics pushed for further studies and proof that the cost and effort required to attain MOL's resolution was worthwhile. In July 1967, facing more scrutiny and tests, Maj. Gen. Stewart expressed, "This is a frustrating exercise. None of the approaches seem to add up to mathematically precise and overwhelming proof that [superior] resolution is a requirement (in lieu of [high] resolution from KH-8). A cost-effectiveness approach seems hopeless – it is easy to compute the cost, but the worth (in dollars) is a highly subjective opinion."[55] MOL's value was indeed subjective, and MOL faced several high-ranking critics. Director of Central Intelligence (DCI) Richard Helms had reservations about the value of MOL's resolution and believed that it simply did not justify the cost of the program.[56] Director of the Defense Intelligence Agency (DIA), Lieutenant General Joseph Carroll, also did not support MOL based on the VHR justification.[57] A 1968 assessment of MOL's unique contributions to national intelligence supported the notion that while VHR would be useful, MOL's costs were not justified based on VHR alone. The study argued, "There is no question that satellite photography with ground resolutions of [superior quality] would provide useful intelligence, especially on technical details of weapon systems."[58] However, the study found, "We have been unable to find potential benefits from the MOL program of sufficient importance to national intelligence alone to justify the expenditures programmed for the future."[59]

In an effort to answer its critics, the MOL Program Office produced a two-volume study titled, "The Value of Very High Resolution Photography" in late 1968.[60] As a whole, "This paper summarizes some of the more significant results thus far of the MOL Program Office effort to express in meaningful terms the value of and need for very high resolution photography."[61] According to the paper, evaluations demonstrated that MOL could provide photography at sufficient resolution for technical intelligence on space targets and make significant contributions to the policing of arms limitation agreements.[62] Looking at relatively recent events, MOL personnel argued, "The MOL has some potential to obtain coverage of targets or areas during periods of international tension and crisis. During the Cuban missile crisis, the value of VHR photography to provide easily understood and incontrovertible evidence for national decision making was clearly demonstrated. MOL will be on orbit about 25 per cent of the time during the year and can pass daily over a point of interest with little penalty."[63] In the course of the two-volume paper, the MOL Program Office argued that MOL's VHR contributions were not limited to pre-planned targets in the Sino-Soviet range, but MOL VHR photography could also contribute to a number of different types of data collection and areas of national security.

Following the study, criticism continued. One internal NRO memorandum from September 1969 stated that although many studies had attempted to make a case for VHR photography, "they have not made a sufficient case to justify MOL is a matter of record."[64] Deputy Assistant Secretary of Defense Ivan Selin summarized the study as stating that MOL's VHR could improve estimates of both Soviet and Chinese forces, allowing the U.S. to plan more conservatively. Additionally, VHR could provide detailed information about the military characteristics of both Soviet and Chinese weapons and permit better design of our weapons, reducing vulnerability and improving effectiveness.[65] But even with these capabilities, Selin argued that VHR was not urgent and there were cheaper alternatives available. Selin explained, "The MOL DCP concludes that the need for VHR imagery is great enough and urgent enough to spend more than $1.5 billion on MOL in FY 69 through FY 71. I do not believe available evidence and analysis support this conclusion."[66]

In the face of widespread criticism, advocates of the program remained. Director of Defense Research and Engineering John S. Foster, Jr. stated, "My conclusion, as presented in the most recent MOL DCP, that the value to DoD of MOL very high resolution photography combined with its mission flexibility justifies the remaining development and estimated operating costs; and my recommendation for proceeding with the baseline (manned and unmanned) program were supported by the Secretary of the Air Force, the President's Scientific Advisor, the Director of the DIA, the Director of the National Reconnaissance Program, and the Assistant Secretary (Comptroller) and approved by the Deputy Secretary of Defense."[67] But even with this impressive list of supporters, MOL continued to be inundated with criticism and skepticism.

The NASA/DoD Overlap

Many skeptics expressed concern regarding potentially duplicative efforts between NASA and DoD programs, despite compromises reached between the two agencies. The biggest hurdle was how these parallel programs were perceived by those on the outside. Due to security constraints, few knew the difference between NASA's Apollo program and the DoD's MOL program. James Abrahamson explained, "NASA was running their [Space Station], which was very confusing, of course. That helped make it a good cover, but Congress and lots of people were asking, 'Wait a minute…' They decided they couldn't hide it so it had to be somewhat out there. NASA had a [Space Station] that was aimed at how long can humans work in space, how well can they do that, what kind of a john do they need, what kind of an exercise program do they need. That was way out there, and a whole group of people were doing those things. So here comes the Air Force in a copy-cat mission, and why is the Air Force doing this?"[68] According to Abrahamson, this perceived overlap was the greatest challenge facing MOL. He argued, "I would say the biggest challenge was when people would say, 'What are you doing?' 'Oh, we're doing human capability in space.' 'But didn't NASA do that?' That was a big problem… Nobody understood what we were, or only a very few congressmen understood what we were trying to do."[69]

A commissioned group published a 25-page report in 1967 which addressed questions regarding the duplicity between the Apollo and MOL programs.[70] Answering the question of whether or not the Apollo Applications Program (AAP) could accomplish MOL's purposes, the report delivered a "qualified yes."[71] Finding the programs to be complimentary instead of competitive, the report argued that achieving MOL's goals via the Apollo program would ultimately be more costly and probably evolve into a single-purpose DoD program. In addition to requiring a number of modifications to Apollo, many feared an Apollo reconnaissance mission would only damage NASA's peaceful image internationally. The report concluded, "In summary, it can be seen that the Apollo Applications Program and MOL Program are different and complementary; they are not competitive in mission and are not redundant in terms of hardware development."[72]

Nonetheless, talk of wasteful duplication and merging the programs persisted. According to one NRO memorandum, "Severe budget limitations in FY 69 plus general Congressional/public criticism of the parallel and apparently duplicative MOL and Orbital Workshop Programs have required that DoD and NASA again assure that the continuation of separate programs is still valid and that the two efforts are as correlated, coordinated, and cost-effective as possible."[73] But MOL's security constraints prevented complete openness with NASA. With so much classified information woven into MOL, "unless the camera system were completely removed, all that NASA will (or could) learn from MOL flights is physiological information on the effects of 30 days weightlessness, and the performance of astronauts in a complex and demanding task (the latter is unique to MOL, and will constitute a significant contribution to the national space program)."[74] Some considered removing the camera for flight 5 (the third manned launch) and diverting it for NASA use. However, given the national urgency and need for MOL's reconnaissance mission, MOL remained high priority.

While both MOL and Apollo were justified as separate programs for the time being, NASA and the DoD did agree to explore ways to reduce expenditures through joint actions. In June 1968, MOL and NASA personnel met to discuss technical details and plans, making it possible for NASA to study ways it could use MOL hardware in their post-Apollo program.[75] DDR&E Foster argued that as both NASA and the DoD faced budget cuts, "The manned spaceflight area, MOL-AAP, appears to have the greatest potential for long term savings."[76] In the following months, collaborative steps were taken between MOL and AAP. MOL Systems Office personnel directly supported and monitored selected activities during the Apollo 7 mission which was launched in October 1968. Additionally, flight crew members and some operations personnel observed simulations and the launch at Cape Kennedy. Of mutual benefit to both programs, MOL Bioastronautics worked with NASA on the mission, offering valuable support to NASA while gaining flight experience for MOL personnel.[77] Although the efforts appeared duplicative from the outside, MOL and AAP supported each other and worked in partnership in valuable ways.

Budget Challenges

According to Robert Crippen, "There were always budget challenges."[78] Budget overages and cuts plagued MOL and ultimately were the biggest factor in its demise. When asked about the Vietnam War's influence on MOL, Richard Truly only saw its impact on MOL's budget. He explained, "The main influence Vietnam had on MOL was it ate up money at an enormous rate. It gave the nation a huge budget problem, and we were a big ticket item."[79] There were a number of competing demands on the nation's budget, and MOL was only one of them. Lachlan Macleay recalled, "The Vietnam War was going on. Lyndon Johnson had his Great Society programs. NASA had their Apollo program. We needed money and the budget, we just kept getting cut and we'd lost $250 million or $150 million.'Ok, let's rearrange things and keep going.' Things just kept slipping. It was strictly money and priorities. Lyndon Johnson's Great Society programs were taking a lot of money, and Apollo was taking a lot of money… We just couldn't keep it going. We had great people, some of the finest people working on that program that I've met in my life. They were really busting their tail to make it work. But if you don't have the money, you can't, you're just stuck. So that's basically what happened."

The first group of crew members started working on MOL the same month the program faced its first budget cut. In November 1965, MOL received word that the Office of the Secretary of Defense was cutting MOL's FY 1967 funding 60%.[80] With such a massive cut, the schedule immediately slipped – delaying the first manned flight at least six months to April 1969.[81] And that was not the only budget discrepancy of that size. In February 1967, MOL personnel met with contractors to mitigate another budget crisis. With a contractor requirement of $811 million for FY 1968 but a budget of only $430 million, the program was forced to again incorporate major schedule slips.[82]

In addition to schedule slips, limited funding also required MOL to consider cutting manpower support from one of its chief contractors, Aerospace.[83] In November 1968, Aerospace Vice President and MOL Division General Manager Walter C. Williams wrote a letter to the MOL Systems Office about the critical problem the funding deficit was creating, explaining, "I am writing you to make you aware of what I consider to be the critical state of Aerospace manpower support to the MOL program. I am bringing this subject to your attention at this point in time because in reviewing the monies allocated to Aerospace support of the program against the manpower which it furnishes as well as a review of our performance to date against those monies, I find there must be some relief in the form of additional funds or we will be faced with a drastic reduction in the manpower that can be applied to MOL and a resultant reduction in technical tasks which we will be able to accomplish."[84] MOL simply did not have enough funds to support the program at its current rate.

> *"I can't seem to refrain from 'selling' MOL."*

By 1968, MOL costs had increased significantly, and the program was now consuming about 17% of the Air Force Research, Development, Test, and Evaluation (RDT&E) budget.[85] Given MOL's overwhelming demand for funding, Air Force leadership was anxious to alleviate the budget strain. However, every budget cut had a significant impact on the program, its schedule, and potentially, its design. In November 1968, John Kirk from the Office of the Director of Defense Research and Engineering indicated "why relatively small budget cuts have so much impact" on such a large program as MOL. Kirk explained that MOL had "no appreciable production base planned," was "stretched very thin financially" and underfunded for both FY 1968 and FY 1969, required a small number of expensive end items which required critical interfaces, and because manpower on the program was at its peak, any budget cut or schedule slip ballooned costs. As one solution, Kirk suggested perhaps the unmanned portion of the program be canceled. The unmanned program had been pushed as a way to avoid international uproar and was expected to be cheaper. But despite the PSAC and State Department fears about the Soviet's reaction to a manned program, the Soviets had accepted the Apollo program and were pursuing their own manned programs. Although the manned program was a little more expensive, it was also more efficient and offered more flexibility. In a note to DNRO Flax directly, despite all the problems MOL was facing, Kirk stated, "I can't seem to refrain from 'selling' MOL."[86]

But not all were convinced that the program was worth its rising cost. In December 1968, DCI Helms argued, "In summary, I continue to feel that MOL-type photography would make a useful contribution to intelligence, but fail to find benefits from the MOL Program of sufficient importance to national intelligence to justify the estimated cost."[87] Other detractors remained unconvinced of MOL's necessity arguing, "The urgency of achieving the objectives of the Manned Orbiting Laboratory Program has never been firmly established. Therefore, a significant funding cutback and the choice to defer the first manned launch by a year or more to reduce the MOL effort to that of optics and payload vehicle technology is not a serious penalty for the Nation."[88] The cost of MOL had more than doubled from its inception. Along with the Apollo program, sending man into space had become a massively expensive endeavor. Some argued, "From the standpoint of our national manned space program there are insufficient benefits to justify the continuation of both programs at a cost of $4 billion ($3 billion MOL and $1 billion AAP)."[89]

The FY 1970 budget was perhaps the most significant budget year to date. At peak manpower, any funding cut would have major repercussions. More than 20% of the entire MOL budget was needed in FY 1970 alone.[90] Facing a swelling budget that was becoming harder to justify, the Bureau of Budget recommended to President Richard Nixon that he terminate MOL only four months into his presidency. Instead of canceling the program immediately, President Nixon requested considering a one-year delay and reducing FY 1970 funding over 30% from $525 million to $360 million.[91] Despite all these objections, many officials remained staunch supporters. DDR&E Foster recommended the program receive its full funding for FY 1970 – at least $525 million.[92] But each budget cut was accompanied by a schedule slip, making the program harder and harder to defend.

MOL's Slipping Schedule

When MOL was announced in August 1965, the program schedule anticipated flying one unmanned qualification flight in 1968, followed by five manned flights beginning later that year. The program was expected to cost $1.5 billion.[93] But the persistent budget crisis wreaked havoc on MOL's schedule. When asked about the schedule slips, Macleay explained, "It was money. It was just flat money."[94] Karol Bobko recalled, "There were a number of times when we had slips because of inadequate funding, and so everybody was worried about that. I can remember one time that they had a study, and it showed that it didn't do any good to slip for less than three months because it took you three months to get squared away after you slipped. And then they slipped for three months."[95] The budget crisis and ensuing schedule slips were seemingly endless. Crippen remembered, "The launch date seemed like it would stay just as far away, every day it didn't get any closer… The challenges were primarily financial."[96] According to the minutes of one MOL Policy Committee meeting from April 1966, the bulk of the meeting was spent discussing funding and schedule slips.[97]

In March 1967, the MOL Systems Office began coordinating with Aerospace and other contractors to rework the schedule and adopt either a 9-month or 12-month schedule slip. Although the 12-month slip allowed for more flexibility, it was also more expensive.[98] After preliminary discussions, leadership determined the 9-month slip was too tight and the 12-month slip too expensive.[99] Instead, hoping to minimize the overhead cost impact, the program office suggested a 15-month slip.[100] In May 1967, after a series of discussions culminating in a meeting between Secretary of the Air Force Brown, DNRO Flax, and Maj. Gen. Stewart, the MOL program adopted a 12-month slip.[101] Over the two years since inception, costs had nearly doubled to $2.8 billion, and they continued to rise. The flight schedule had been reconfigured to add a second unmanned qualification flight, and incorporating the concurrent development plan for manned and unmanned capabilities, MOL was now scheduled to fly three manned missions and two unmanned missions. Managing the changes to the flight schedule and increased program cost, the first qualification flight was now expected to fly in December 1970 and the first manned flight was expected for August 1971, with the first unmanned flight expected over a year after that.[102] In two years of development, the MOL schedule had slipped two years. The schedule adjustments did not stop there. By the end of 1967, MOL had incorporated another schedule slip, this one for 13 weeks.[103]

Although a major contributor, funding was not the only issue causing program delays. A MOL Program Review Committee meeting was held in November 1967 in an effort to move MOL onto sound financial footing and address the scheduling concerns. According to meeting minutes, six months after adopting the 12-month slip, "Eastman Kodak Company [EKC] has admitted that it could never have met the compact 12 schedule. This inability is a result not of lack of funding support but the fact that EKC's technical and production competence, independent of funding, cannot support our present schedules. They are now offering a compact 12 + 12 i.e., a two year slip to the baseline program, as their capability, at an increase in cost to $491 million." Discussing these complications, "General Martin commented that the program slippage appeared to him to be so great that it probably would be cheaper and quicker to go to an unmanned development program effort, and that the [superior] capability could probably be attained without man, using the program vehicle. Dr. Flax's reply was to the effect that if EKC is the pacing element, General Martin's suggestion might not be valid. If there were fund limitations but EKC was not pacing, then General Martin's suggestion might be right." Costs escalated three times during 1967, and DNRO Flax expressed concern that "We may be rapidly pricing the program out of business." However, he claimed the Eastman Kodak delays were "the real key to our problem."[104]

The year 1967 was challenging for MOL, and the problems were not solved by the end of the year. In a memorandum for the Secretary of the Air Force, General Ferguson explained, "Since early in calendar year 1967, the MOL Program has been engaged in a continuing effort to achieve a realistic balance among program scope, schedules, and funding for the Engineering Development Phase of the MOL System." Despite efforts to address the problems, General Ferguson noted, "The above factors have now combined to create a situation in which existing program scope and schedules are altogether inconsistent with anticipated funding levels."[105]

Talk of further schedule slips persisted, and MOL leadership feared for the program's future. In June 1968, Maj. Gen. Stewart wrote to DNRO Flax regarding the upcoming funding and schedule situation. Explaining that with fewer funds available for FY 1969, it was impossible for MOL to avoid slipping the first manned launch from August 1971 to sometime in 1972, subsequently increasing costs to over $3 billion. Maj. Gen. Stewart warned, "In my opinion, this will result in the program position being even more precarious than it is already." As a solution, Maj. Gen. Stewart suggested deferring the unmanned program and pursuing two unmanned qualification launches followed by four manned launches, with the first manned launch in November 1971. Maj. Gen. Stewart argued, "Past circumstances and decisions have led to the current situation wherein the program apparently cannot be stretched-out further in any reasonably efficient manner." Maj. Gen. Stewart also feared another major delay could strengthen critics' arguments and "place it [MOL] in even greater jeopardy than it is at present – if that is possible."[106] MOL personnel and contractors met in July 1968 to discuss the upcoming budget reduction and schedule impact. According to Lieutenant Colonel Bertram Kemp from MOL, "In my view, almost no progress toward arriving at a realistic and acceptable schedule had been made." Facing yet another six-month slip, the situation was becoming more and more dire. According to Kemp, "There seemed to be a consensus among many who had attended previous rescheduling meetings that this meeting was proving to be the most difficult."[107]

The frequent schedule slips proved damaging to the MOL crew members. Albert Crews recalled of 1968, "After we'd been there three years, it was still as long to fly as it was when we started."[108] Macleay also noted the frustration and explained, "We were having some morale problems because we were all hard-charging and wanted to get going, and the damn program kept slipping. I think we went at least two years without gaining a day. We'd say, 'Well the only thing constant on the program was the number of days until the first launch.' We were just treading water."[109] Truly recalled, "We used to joke about it, that every year we were still three years from flight."[110] Facing little progress toward launch, Crews explained, "Of our first group, two guys quit."[111] In July 1966, Michael Adams was the first to leave the program. John Finley was the second crew member to leave MOL, returning to the Navy in April 1968.

By the end of 1968, the MOL program office had adjusted the schedule yet again; the qualification flights were now expected in December 1970 and July 1971, with the first manned flight anticipated in December 1971.[112] Facing delay after delay, support for MOL waned. Abrahamson explained, "The real problem was we had delays, and that's why the program was canceled. The unmanned surveillance program through the NRO was just going ahead very effectively. Ours had to develop all this astronaut business and what we could contribute. I think there was genuinely and perhaps warranted skepticism about that. That competition we felt very significantly."[113] The manned MOL program, despite unquestionable talent and significant potential contributions, was taking too long.

Justifying MOL

Originally, the Department of Defense pursued the MOL concept and President Johnson authorized its development because, according to early studies, MOL was the simplest and most reliable method of obtaining superior resolution photographs for the longest possible duration.[114] A 1967 paper titled "Basis for Confidence in Achieving the Objectives of MOL" outlined what MOL personnel were doing to ensure the success of the program: designing conservatively, building precise tools for test and manufacture, building an adequate and orderly program schedule, and incorporating man to capitalize on capabilities for success and improvement.[115] But MOL faced a myriad of problems and criticisms from the very beginning, forcing advocates to remain continually on the defense.

MOL Technical Director Michael Yarymovych explained the situation in late 1967, "When the MOL program was approved at the level of $1.5 billion, it was to be a six-flight program (one unmanned test; five manned) which had as its primary purpose the optical reconnaissance mission, but also contained secondary military and tertiary objectives. At that time it was difficult to conceive of an automatic mode of conducting the reconnaissance task. The entire payload job was estimated to cost about $500 million. At the present, we have a program whose total price is near $3 billion and which has only a single principal objective. The payload cost now is estimated at about $1 billion. The role of man is questionable. Because of the sole identification of the program with the reconnaissance mission, there is very little actual support from the Air Force. Conversely, the price for achieving very high resolution is becoming so high that the reconnaissance community is dubious about the worth."[116]

In spite of all these concerns – rising costs, questionable support, and other problems – Yarymovych and others believed the program remained essential. Yarymovych concluded his memorandum, "I believe it is of vital interest to our national defense to maintain the MOL manned capability, regardless of possible inefficiencies which are inherent in an underfunded budget."[117] Many of those involved in the program and knowledgeable of its mission believed deeply in MOL's worth. Macleay explained, "We had a mission to do. It was good for the country. It was going to help things that needed to be done, going to give a capability that had never been there before. Man, I was all for it. I had no concerns about the program at all, other than how long it was going to take."[118]

However, the nature of MOL's reconnaissance mission and its strict security complicated matters, especially when trying to garner support and funding from Congress. In material prepared for Congressional hearings regarding FY 1970, MOL documents highlighted how difficult it was to justify MOL to a full congressional committee without referencing the reconnaissance mission.[119] The MOL program office explained, "Greater scrutiny than ever is anticipated this year considering the general mood of Congress concerning defense costs and spending on space programs in general... Again this year, another adjustment in the MOL schedule must be reported as well as a major program change (from seven to six launches). This latter change will probably generate considerable interest. Intense questioning on NASA-DoD duplication is also expected, particularly with regard to any future space program plans, including merger of DoD and NASA projects. There are also indications that the value of MOL in relation to its cost may be seriously questioned. This, of course, will be extremely difficult to answer in full committee sessions."[120]

As predicted, congressional hearings in front of full committees proved challenging. In a meeting of the House Armed Services Committee in May of 1969, several committee members raised questions about MOL.[121] When members of the committee were informed that only four members, designated by the Chairman, had full access to information on MOL, several members demanded to know more.[122] It was a challenging balance between transparency in order to gain support and secrecy to protect highly sensitive information. A MOL briefing policy paper from the time explained the problem, "It is questionable as to whether we can gain and/or maintain the necessary interest in and support for the MOL program among concerned Congressional, military and professional groups and still adhere to currently exercised security policy and briefing procedures."[123] MOL personnel suggested several solutions including officially canceling the program and moving it to completely black security classification, broadening the black base, developing the white objectives, and changing the security classification.[124] Ultimately, the lack of transparency contributed to the program's cancellation. Abrahamson explained, "I think the fact that we couldn't explain and justify what we were doing was a factor" in the demise of the program.[125]

In January 1969, President Richard Nixon was sworn in as President. Under a new administration, MOL faced new scrutiny, and supporters were trying to save it. In his role as Deputy Director of Space Systems in the Pentagon, Brigadier General Lew Allen, Jr. explained, "At this time the program is being reviewed and judged on the basis of an operational reconnaissance program in direct competition for intelligence gathering assets."[126] Recognizing the gravity of the situation, Allen highlighted MOL's significant contributions – data on man's utility for reconnaissance and military purposes, a qualified optical system with advanced performance, VHR photography, and becoming the basis for future manned and VHR programs.[127] Making a case for itself, the Program Office produced a condensed version of the November 1968 report, "The Need for Very High Resolution Imagery" now titled "Mission Value."[128]

Richard M. Nixon.
Source: CSNR Reference Collection.

Lew Allen, Jr..
Source: CSNR Reference Collection.

John L. McLucas.
Source: CSNR Reference Collection.

MOL vehicle assembly. Source: CSNR Reference Collection.

In addition to justifying MOL's existence, supporters also emphasized that MOL was on track and progressing. Maj. Gen. Bleymaier conducted a briefing with the new DNRO John McLucas in April 1969 emphasizing "that the program was on schedule, that there were no technical problems, progress was measurable, management tools and relationships between the government and contractors are adequate and satisfactory."[129] Despite a myriad of challenges and criticisms, supporters continued to advocate for the program and MOL continued.

MOL astronaut training. Source: CSNR Reference Collection.

MOL Continues

By mid-1968, MOL's engineering and development work was going smoothly, and things seemed to finally be falling into place. As of January 1969, SLC-6, the MOL launch facility at Vandenberg Air Force Base, was slated for completion in April of that year.[130] In February, the Program Office held several sign-off meetings in order to clean up the "to be determined" and "to be resolved" issues. In one meeting, 227 items were submitted, and 213 items were approved.[131] Additionally, the MOL Program Office reported that personnel were making considerable progress on the Laboratory Module and software.[132] That month the Air Force's Space Launch Office suggested that MOL crew members begin to familiarize themselves with intelligence targets and complexes likely to be Dorian targets. The final list they were to study included 61 installations in the Soviet Union and Communist China which were of extreme interest to the United States.[133]

But criticism continued from the outside, prompting some changes to the program's scope and design. Facing schedule slips and budget constraints, Maj. Gen. Stewart briefed DNRO Flax in June 1968 and suggested MOL cancel the unmanned portion of the program.[134] That was one solution to a large problem. In December, DDR&E Foster explained the situation, "MOL is the largest program element in the RDTE budget and continuing concern is expressed by Bureau of the Budget and others regarding total program cost and annual funding levels required to support the program. In addition, the Air Force has given serious consideration to elimination of the unmanned capability for MOL." Given the state of the program, Foster divided the problem into three questions. First, should MOL be canceled? Second, if the program were to continue, should the unmanned system be canceled? Lastly, if the program were to continue, what should the financial support to the program look like for FY 1970? Exploring these issues, Foster argued that MOL's mission flexibility and VHR contributions – including monitoring arms limitation agreements and obtaining coverage of targets during times of crisis – justified MOL and its expenses. With that said, Foster recommended that MOL be funded its full amount of $575 million for FY 1970 and the unmanned option remain part of MOL.[135]

The issue was not put to rest, however. Three months later, in March 1969, newly-appointed Deputy Secretary of Defense David Packard signed the order to proceed with a four-launch manned-only MOL schedule.[136] On 1 April 1969, the MOL Program Office received the order and Maj. Gen. Stewart informed Maj. Gen. Bleymaier that they were to stop all effort toward the unmanned system, which was now deferred until at least FY 1972.[137] This change was not met with universal approval. The PSAC Panel had always privately favored an exclusively unmanned MOL program, but had officially complied with MOL's concurrent development strategy for both manned and unmanned systems.[138] When the panel received word that the unmanned portion of the system had been put on hold for at least two years, they were "quite disturbed."[139] In response, the panel offered several suggestions that would make the unmanned system feasible earlier and urged leadership to explore the options.

By May 1969, the MOL Program Office was making a case for its FY 1970 funding. Having suffered through funding instability during 1967, 1968, and 1969, the program's contractors needed stabilized funding for at least the next two years in order to complete the hardware development.[140] The Program Office argued that management had repeatedly demonstrated their ability to effectively manage funds and tightly control allocations. The MOL program, with its adjusted schedule, was completely defined and each element of the schedule could be met; it just needed $525 million in FY 1970 and a firm commitment for the FY 1971 funding.[141] Arguing that the program's budget had accrued over $600 million in additional costs due to forced program slips, the program was now at a tipping point, and it was essential that government leaders commit to funding the program.[142]

Talk of Cancellation

During the May 1969 budget conversations, General Ferguson stated, "We are ready to fish or cut bait."[143] Unfortunately for MOL, many felt it was time to "cut bait." In February 1969, Robert Mayo, the newly-appointed Director of the Office of Management and Budget (OMB), suggested reviewing the three large DoD space programs – MOL, Hexagon, and drones – in order to look for potential savings. The Bureau of the Budget (BoB) found MOL to be too expensive and of questionable significance. The BoB argued that MOL's contributions were quickly becoming obsolete with new technological advancements, particularly with the Gambit-3 system in development, stating, "Since 1965-1966 when the decision was made to pursue the MOL for its intelligence value, the relative benefit and the cost of the MOL have changed very significantly." Citing the ballooning costs from its original $1.5 billion price tag to its current $3.2 billion projected cost, the BoB argued that MOL's VHR contributions were simply not enough to justify the cost.[144] According to the BoB, it was time to cancel MOL.

Responding to the BoB's paper, the MOL Program Office claimed the Budget Bureau's total savings estimate of $2 billion between FY 1969 and 1970 was unrealistic.[145] The Program Office also argued that, at a resolution better or comparable to Gambit-3, MOL had much to contribute to the country's intelligence gathering.[146] Although the Assistant Secretary of Defense for Systems Analysis, Ivan Selin, generally agreed with the BoB's opinion on MOL, identifying the complexities of the situation, the Selin argued, "Other considerations than intelligence apply: appeal of man in space; large sunk costs in MOL. Terminating MOL [is an] unrealistic option."[147] Instead of terminating MOL, the Science Advisor suggested re-exploring the option of combining MOL with the Apollo Applications Program, recognizing that the agencies preferred to maintain their separate programs and that there were both domestic and international concerns regarding a militarization of NASA.[148]

In February 1969, amid major budget negotiations and after some critics suggested it was time to cancel MOL, Robert C. Seamans, Jr. succeeded Harold Brown as Secretary of the Air Force. Immediately upon appointment, Seamans entered the MOL conversation with a memorandum to the Deputy Secretary of Defense in which he suggested several alternatives to the current program.[149] Exploring both a three-flight and four-fight plan, Seamans weighed costs and impact to schedule. Ultimately, with the support of Dr. Foster and Dr. Flax, Seamans recommended pursuing a four-flight plan. Seamans argued the four-flight plan "would protect, with minimum commitment, until December 1970 a continuing very high resolution operational reconnaissance capability in the 1970s, provide time in which to carefully assess other options, and sustain a minimum cost development program leading to manned or unmanned operational systems."[150] Seamans and others hoped this solution would save MOL.

Unfortunately, MOL's problems were not over. The following month, Maj. Gen. Stewart reported to Dr. Seamans that he expected MOL to be funded at least $85 million under their stated need, if it survived the current BoB issue, causing yet another schedule slip of at least six months. Lamenting MOL's budget history, Stewart stated, "When the past history of MOL is reviewed, it is difficult to be optimistic about the future." Stewart explained the massive role continual underfunding had on the program, "At the $556 million level in FY 70, and assuming adequate future-year financial support, the first manned launch in the MOL program will take place at least 27 months behind the initial Phase II target date of December 1969. Approximately half of those 27 lost months can be attributed to inadequate funding."[151] Due to the current state of the program with hardware development and peak contractor manpower, even minor fund reductions had a disproportionately large impact on

Robert C. Seamans, Jr..
Source: CSNR Reference Collection.

Melvin R. Laird.
Source: CSNR Reference Collection.

schedule slips and overall increases to program cost. Frustrated by the perpetual budget crisis, Stewart stated, "MOL history and current financial discussions indicate that we either will be unable or unwilling to fund the program properly. And if that is a correct assessment of future prospects, then we should face the facts and terminate MOL now."[152]

By April 1969, MOL had been engaged in this cycle of being underfunded, adjusting its schedule, and requiring more money for four years. Maj. Gen. Stewart and new Secretary of Defense Melvin R. Laird sent drafted memorandums, intended for the new President, to Dr. Seamans addressing the situation. In Maj. Gen. Stewart's memorandum, he stated, "I recommend a reorientation of this program as follows: We should continue to develop the MOL camera system as part of an unmanned, covert satellite system in the National Reconnaissance Program. We should cancel all elements of the overt Manned Orbiting Laboratory Program and announce that we are doing this partly to conserve funds, partly because the program has slipped 2 ½ years since first start, and partly because we can now pursue many of the original objectives with less expensive, unmanned systems."[153] After highlighting the need for VHR photography and many of man's contributions to the program design, Stewart stated, "I reluctantly conclude that we should pursue an optimized unmanned configuration."[154] Canceling the manned portion of MOL entailed a myriad of consequences including massive layoffs at a number of contractor sites and, in order to protect the secrecy of the NRO, a public announcement of program cancellation. After corresponding with Dr. Seamans, Maj. Gen. Stewart observed to General Ferguson, "[The] MOL Program is on shakier ground than it ever has been before. Dr. Seamans clearly does not want MOL terminated, but recognizes it may become a dollar casualty."[155]

In his memorandum to the President, Secretary of Defense Laird recommended that the administration should either fund MOL at a level commensurate with reasonable progress or terminate the overt manned program and continue with the VHR camera system.[156] Laird pointed out that by the end of FY 1969, the government will have invested approximately $1.23 billion in MOL since the program began in September 1966. Laird argued that with a history of underfunding and schedule slips driving up overall costs, the administration needed to explore options. Balancing program costs, the benefits of VHR, and the potential added capabilities by including man, Laird stated that the "potential value [is] sufficient that we should continue to pursue this capability either in the MOL or an unmanned satellite using the MOL camera."[157]

Facing further underfunding, in the May 1969 MOL Policy Committee Meeting, General Ferguson urged the Committee to either fund the program or terminate it.[158] Eventually MOL crew members heard rumors of his comment, though many were unaware of who said it. Crippen recalled, "I was told at one time that one of the Air Force generals that was over MOL back in Washington had finally told the Bureau [of Budget] that because the program kept stretching out, he said, 'If you really want us to do it, give us the money and go do it. But if you don't, cancel the program.'"[159]

Months after the BoB's February recommendation to terminate MOL, the MOL Program Office and other advocates were still responding. On 17 May 1969, President Nixon met with Secretary Laird, Secretary Seamans, Maj. Gen. Stewart, Dr. Henry Kissinger in his capacity as National Security Advisor, OMB Director Mayo, and Assistant Director of the Bureau of the Budget James R. Schlesinger to discuss MOL and allow the Department of Defense to provide a counter-case to the Budget Bureau's proposal to terminate.[160] The Defense Department representatives explained that MOL currently had 19,000 associate contractors on board, with approximately 65,000 contractors involved in total. By that time, about $1.3 billion had been invested in the program with another $1.9 billion expected in costs. Most importantly, the Department of Defense argued that the manned MOL system offered the highest confidence for the best possible photography during the President's tenure.[161] Dr. Seamans stated that canceling MOL would be a "bitter pill" to swallow for both the Air Force in general and for him personally.[162]

Under the direction of Lt. Col. Larry Skantze, MOL personnel prepared a 34-page paper in early June which highlighted MOL's successes and future potential.[163] The Program Office stated, "The MOL Program is currently progressing well. It is totally defined, and all engineering is understood... The Program is meeting all schedule dates, and detailed test results of critical components indicate that system performance specifications required to meet the [superior] resolution goal will be met or exceeded."[164] According to the Program Office, MOL was on schedule for its first manned launch in July 1972, the "achievement of all MOL Program objectives is highly predictable, and the system will provide a dramatic increase in the quality and value of satellite reconnaissance. Performance of the MOL crew will establish a wealth of basic understanding, in quantitative terms, of what enhancement and flexibility man can bring to military space operations."[165] MOL was viable, the "keystone" upon which Defense Department space goals would be constructed over the next decade. In addition, it held great potential for longer missions, better resolution, enhanced payloads, new experiments, and even partnership with future Space Transportation Systems.[166]

While MOL personnel worked diligently to justify the program, others moved ahead with plans in case of cancellation. On 6 June 1969, DDR&E Foster and Secretary Seamans addressed the real possibility of termination by stating, "The DoD faces severe pressures to reduce both FY 1970 and out-year costs. If we can severely curtail or abandon one or more large costly R&D programs, we can avoid paralyzing a great number of smaller ones. Consequently we have considered alternatives to the current MOL program."[167] According to the Air Force, the three alternatives were to proceed with the present manned-only program, develop a new unmanned system using MOL's camera system, or terminate all MOL activities and delay developing a photographic reconnaissance satellite system that provides a superior resolution. Due to insufficient funding but the real need for VHR, Foster and Seamans recommended the program continue in a less capable but adequate unmanned system.[168] Foster and Seamans suggested all preliminary steps be taken, and the program could be officially canceled by close of business on 10 June 1969.[169]

Terminating MOL

After four years, MOL was officially terminated on Tuesday, 10 June 1969. In a letter from the Department of the Air Force Plans Group dated 10 June, Colonel John Shaughnessy stated, "MOL termination should not be construed as a reflection on the Air Force. The MOL goals were practical and achievable; maximum benefit was being taken of hardware and experience from NASA and other DoD space projects; and the program was well-managed and good progress was being made. Under other circumstances, its continuation would have been fully justified."[170] MOL was undoubtedly a casualty of its circumstances.

Although the program was canceled on 10 June, word had begun to spread the weekend prior. Maj. Gen. Stewart notified Maj. Gen. Bleymaier on Saturday, 7 June, "The 'administration' (presumably the President) has decided to terminate MOL except for the 'Automatic' camera system. This, of course, is a public termination of the entire MOL program. I gather the plan is for Secretary Laird to announce MOL termination in Congress at 1030 AM Tuesday; the Air Force to notify MOL contractors at the same time, and Mr. Packard to hold a press conference on the termination at about 1100 AM in the Pentagon also on Tuesday."[171] According to Maj. Gen. Stewart, public announcements and statements would claim both the need to further reduce federal defense spending and advancements in automated techniques for unmanned satellite systems led to the program's demise. In essence, although MOL was worthwhile, it simply did not equate in immediate value to the sum of the other DoD programs.[172]

Maj. Gen. Stewart also prepared Maj. Gen. Bleymaier for the immediate aftermath. He warned, "When the news breaks, you will be deluged with queries. Other than informal responses to primary MOL contractors, all queries should be referred to SAFOI or MOL Program Office."[173] According to Maj. Gen. Stewart, most of the work on MOL would be terminated immediately. Because work on the facility at Vandenberg Air Force Base was already well underway, construction would be completed to a minimum practical extent and then mothballed for possible future use. He continued, "Unless some miracle happens, Col Kemp will be out Sunday PM with the official direction to terminate, stop work, or reduce effort in line with the preceding sections."[174]

Facing impending cancellation, a document prepared by NRO personnel on 8 June outlined the history of the MOL program, and its persistent budget problems and schedule slips, concluding, "In summary, the MOL Program was underfunded by more than $100 million in Fiscal Years 1968 and 1969, and would have been underfunded about that much in FY 1970."[175] It was also found, "At least half of the stretch-out and cost increase was attributable solely to underfunding."[176] But recognizing the role underfunding played in the demise of the program was not enough to turn it around. On 9 June, Deputy Secretary of Defense David Packard informed Secretary of the Air Force Seamans and DNRO McLucas that the Air Force was to terminate MOL.[177]

> *"They just turned around and went home."*

As planned, the Secretary of Defense announced MOL's termination on 10 June 1969. Although the budget battles and schedule slips had been going on for years, the program's cancellation was still shocking to many. Karol Bobko recalled, "When they canceled the program, they called everybody into the auditorium and just said, 'It's canceled.'"[178] Bobko was shocked and went on to say, "I don't know what happened. I think it surprised everybody. I thought that when it was canceled, we had a fairly good mission, and we were really starting to work towards our goal. And then it was canceled out of the blue."[179] Robert Crippen recalled similar shock over the announcement. He explained that he was "flabbergasted. I couldn't believe it. I was getting up to go to work one morning, and I think I was just shaving when the phone rang. It was our secretary in the office, a lady by the name of Kris Winegarden. She said, 'Crip, the program's canceled.' None of us saw it coming. It was out of the blue from our standpoint and probably one of the low points in my life. After just being selected to be an astronaut, even though it was a classified program, to not know what I was going to be doing in the future, was one of the low points. We held what we called MOL wakes in the officer's club there every afternoon after work."[180] According to Macleay, "Some of the guys were driving up the freeway, on their way to work, and the radio comes on, and a couple of them just turned around and went home. They just turned around and went home."[181]

Several of the crew members were at other locations doing site work when the program was canceled. Abrahamson recalled, "There were four of us up at Vandenberg. We had taken T-38's and flown up to Vandenberg. We were looking at SLC-6 Space Launch, which was the pad that was being converted for the launch of the MOL bird, and the work that was being done on the ground support building, huge building with simulators and other activities which was really going to be a major center for the effort. We were up checking on the progress. This guy comes running up, 'The program has been canceled.' We couldn't believe it. Terrible."[182]

Macleay and Truly were both at GE on 10 June. Macleay recalled, "Dick and I were back at General Electric at an interface control working group. It was the final meeting of the interface control working group, and it was going to be a two-day meeting. At the end of the second day, one of the guys was having a big barbeque for everybody at his house. Anyway, about 9:30 or 10 o'clock in the morning, the meeting had been starting and I got a poke and said, 'Hey, Walt Casey wants to talk to you.' I got on the phone and he said, 'There's word came in here that the program has been canceled.' I said, 'Well is it official?' He said, 'I don't know, that's just what I heard.' So I called Dick in the other room and told him and said, 'Let's just keep doing what we're doing until somebody tells us not to.' What can I say, about half an hour later, here comes the president of General Electric with his secretary, she's crying, and he announces the program is canceled. Dick and I weren't sure what to do. I'd never been in a big cancellation; I didn't know what to do, he didn't know what to do."[183]

Truly similarly remembered, "We were in a SCIF up at GE in King of Prussia, and I was sitting at a table arguing with a guy who I think worked for McDonnell Douglas. We were arguing, literally, over a bit in a software program. We were arguing about the smallest piece of the space program, a single line of code in Gemini. I can't even remember what it was. Anyway, I was sitting there arguing this, it was about 10 in the morning, and Mac walked in the conference room and tapped me on the shoulder. I looked up at him and I said, 'Wait a minute, back up, I'm about to win this argument.' He jabbed my shoulder and I looked around to him and he said, 'The program is canceled.' I looked at him, and I knew Mac well enough that I knew it was true. I looked back at this guy I had been arguing with, I couldn't even remember what the argument was about. And it was gone. It was over."[184]

When they returned to the MOL office the following day, Truly recalled, "It was like a morgue. It was like utter shock. It wasn't just the crew, it was everybody. The NRO people in the program office, the Air Force people, the secretaries, it was just total shock. Then of course for the crew guys, particularly for the Navy guys, we didn't have a job. We didn't know what we were going to go do. It was June 10th, it was Tuesday. We still refer to it as Black Tuesday."[185] Macleay echoed the surprise they all felt and explained, "It was a surprise to me. I had no idea that it was going to be canceled. I didn't even know it was under consideration. Evidently it had been for some time. Melvin Laird was the Defense Secretary at the time, and I think he tried to save it. It was not successful."[186]

Al Crews expressed less shock than others over the program's cancellation explaining, "As I said before, I kind of guessed because it made sense. I mean since I knew that the purpose of us was to back up the manned system in case it didn't work, and it was obvious that it was working great. So unless they came back and let us do the Skylab or something, there was nothing to look forward to. Then every time somebody turned around, new money, new anything, went to NASA, it didn't go to the Air Force. It seemed like the President was saying, 'We don't want any military association with our astronaut program.' It was just the wrong time."[187] According to Crews, "Looking back now, it's obvious that our country had decided to put everything into the civilian part of the space program. MOL was canceled; its obvious reason was because there was no requirement for us. Unmanned systems did just as good, probably better, than we could have ever done. But we were good enough to do what they needed."[188]

Although Crippen felt man could not be completely replaced by the unmanned systems, he did agree with Crews that the unmanned systems were fiercely competitive. He explained, "It was true that unmanned systems were advancing very rapidly. They were coming up with capabilities to actually transmit data down as opposed to having to get film carried down. That, I think, might have posed some problems when people were looking at the picture of technology – was it necessary to go invest in what we were doing as opposed to waiting on some of this newer technology to come on board… Although I think even with the capability to transmit data down, having humans on board could lead to enhancement of what we were getting."[189]

For Macleay, although the unmanned technology was advancing, cancellation was all about the money. He explained, "The official explanation, I think, was just money. We weren't getting there, and their priorities were too many other priorities for money, we weren't getting it. But there were other hints going around that the technology was advancing at the point where… automatic image motion compensation and other sensors, they could do it without us. But as far as I was concerned, it was just money. We just ran out of time, ran out of money, we weren't getting there. Because we weren't getting any closer to the launch, they were just kind of pouring money down a rat hole, as far as they were concerned. We weren't getting there, and the money was eating up too much."[190]

The frustration for many was rooted in the fact that the program had finally seemed to find its footing. Regarding the Dorian payload, "Eastman Kodak had made impressive progress on the facilities, flight hardware, and ground test equipment required to fulfill the objectives of the Dorian Program. At the time of termination they were essentially on schedule with all elements of the program, although there were some minor slippages on the order of 2-4 months."[191] Although the program had been plagued by delays, Crippen recalled, "Toward the end, actually, I thought we were doing pretty good."[192] Truly and Macleay were working the targeting software and were finally making real progress just prior to cancellation. Truly remembered, "We were unsuccessful for a long time, but in the late spring of 1969, Eureka, we had it! We had it. There was a competition for who would code the software. TRW ended up winning it. Then the program was canceled… That is exactly how I remember it, is that we had just been failing, failing, failing to work all this out, and we finally did and we had a competition to select a targeting software contractor, and the program was canceled."[193] Truly went on, "I think we finally had gotten to the point where those problems had ironed out. I honestly believe at the time the program was canceled, we really were going to start marching to a schedule by that time."[194] After working for years on MOL and finally having major breakthroughs, MOL's cancellation was devastating to all who were involved.

MOL's Termination and its People

At the time of termination, a total of 192 military personnel and 100 civilians were assigned between east and west coast MOL activities.[195] Within weeks of program termination, 80% of the approximately 180 officers and airmen assigned to the MOL System Office were given firm immediate or future assignments. Approximately 100 MOL civilian personnel were reassigned to SAMSO.[196] By the end of November, only 10 military personnel and 16 civilians remained with the MOL program.[197] On 10 June 1969, 13,187 contractor personnel were cleared on MOL and faced reassignment. Facilitating the termination, Colonel Fred Dietrich was appointed Termination Contracting Officer (TCO) for MOL in June, while his vice, Thomas Rutter, Deputy Director of Procurement and Production, was appointed on 1 July.[198]

Prior to termination, Michael Adams, John Finley, and Robert Lawrence had already left the program. But in June 1969, there were still fourteen MOL crew members who were working toward flying in space – something many aspired to from childhood. Now many of them were unsure about what to do next. According to Crippen, "We still had our regular weekly pilot meetings, trying to figure out what we could do, lamenting the fact that the program had been canceled. One day Bo [Bobko] said, 'Why don't we ask NASA if they could use us?' We all poo-pooed that idea. This was '69 and Apollo 11 just went to the moon, but NASA was already starting to cancel some downstream Apollo missions. We said, 'They don't have any work for us. There's no chance they're going to take us.' But one thing led to another, and I don't think it was our discussion, but MOL did ask NASA if they could use any of our resources, including some of the crew."[199]

Despite NASA cutbacks, MOL crew members flew to Houston to meet with NASA leadership and discuss transferring. Crippen explained, "We all ended up going down to Houston to be interviewed by Deke Slayton who was one of the original Mercury 7 and who was head of the flight crew operations at the time. Deke said, 'Hey, I don't need you. I've got more people than I know what to do with, and they're canceling flights on me already.' But one thing led to another, and one of the big bosses at NASA in Washington, a guy by the name of George Miller, he ended up telling Deke and folks at Houston that they should at least take some of them. We were fourteen crew members at that time. Deke said, 'Ok, I'll take everybody that's 35 and younger.' I happened to be on the lucky side of that."[200] Truly recalled a similar experience, stating, "There were fourteen crew on the MOL. I think all but one, Bob Herres, said they wanted to go to NASA. NASA didn't need us. But we flew down and had a meeting with Deke Slayton who ran flight crew operations. Deke was very honest; I mean he said it wasn't personal. He said, 'I don't need you. We're flying Apollo, and we've got so many seats. I've got more people down here that are already training for it. Go away.' Eventually the solution was that they took the seven youngest. I was the only one of the original crew selection that was still young enough to be in the seven youngest of the 14."[201]

> *All seven MOL crew members who transferred to NASA eventually flew on the space shuttle.*

Following negotiations, NASA took the seven youngest MOL crew members – Richard Truly, Karol Bobko, Robert Crippen, C. Gordon Fullerton, Henry Hartsfield, Robert Overmyer, and Donald Peterson. Crippen recalled, "Seven of us ended up reporting to NASA. We didn't go through any kind of selection at all, we walked in the door and started working. Deke said, 'Hey, I don't have any flights for you until something they're calling the space shuttle, which is an approved program, might be built. That'll probably be around 1980 or so.' But he said, 'I've got lots of work for you to do.'"[202] All seven MOL crew members who transferred to NASA eventually flew on the space shuttle.

Some of those who qualified for the transfer to NASA chose to delay a year in favor of furthering their education. Bobko explained, "The first thing I decided was if I were going to go back into the Air Force, I should go get my master's. Everybody seemed to be very amenable to let us do that, anything we wanted. I had applied through the Air Force to go to USC, and I was in that pipeline to do that when NASA said they would like to take basically the younger half of the MOL crew members. Everybody agreed, both NASA and the Air Force, you guys should be allowed to go to school for a year. There were a couple of us that did that, Don Peterson and Hank Hartsfield and myself. We all

The seven MOL pilots who transferred to NASA.
From left to right: Bobko, Fullerton, Hartsfield, Crippen, Peterson, Truly, Overmyer. Source: CSNR Reference Collection.

went to school for the year, I got my master's degree. You'll see with us, different people will have us joining NASA at different times because most everybody went in '69, and I didn't go until '70."[203]

On the other side of the age divide, Macleay recalled, "Now NASA really didn't need any more people. But evidently, they reluctantly agreed to take on some. So we all went down for interviews. It started off in the morning, I think, with a big briefing by Deke Slayton at which time he pointed out that if you were 35 years old or older, you might want to think about doing something else. And of course I was 38. I didn't think I wanted to go down there anyway, to tell you the truth. Then in the afternoon, we went in for individual interviews, I guess you could call them interviews, with Deke Slayton. I think I kind of surprised him because I walked in and said, 'This will be a very short interview because I don't want to come down here.' I remember this to this day, I said, 'But I'll tell you there are two guys on this flight crew that if you don't take them, you're crazy.' And he said, 'Who are they?' I said, 'They're Dick Truly and Bob Crippen.' They were two of my closest friends and really great, great people. And they both ended up being very successful there."[204]

Al Crews was also on the wrong side of the age divide and explained, "By that time I was 40, so I wasn't even close... I went to Houston, hoping that I would get a break. But it was obvious that they had more people selected than they had things for."[205] Although he was not able to transfer as an astronaut, Crews did work at NASA. He recalled, "When I got there, there was a flight crew support office that I was put in... I was working on the Skylab, and I did that about a year. Then they opened up the shuttle program office, and I got assigned over to it."[206] Macleay reflected on Crews' later career, "He went to flight test at NASA and was very influential down there in developing various shuttle things."[207]

Abrahamson missed NASA's age cutoff too, but just barely. He recalled, "I had turned 36 two months before. I went down and talked to everybody I could at NASA, and they said, 'Well, right behind you is another one and then another one behind that. If we make the exception for you, I know two months is hard, but that's the cut-off.' So I didn't get to do it. But I got to go run the shuttle program."[208] Abrahamson enjoyed a productive career, later transferring to the National Aeronautics and Space Council and eventually running the new Strategic Defense Initiative (SDI) under President Reagan.

Richard Lawyer returned to the Flight Test School at Edwards Air Force Base, retiring as a colonel in 1982. Lachlan Macleay earned his MBA from USC and returned to active duty in the Air Force, retiring in 1978. Francis Neubeck also returned to active duty, retiring as a colonel in 1986. James Taylor returned to active duty, flying out of the Test Pilot School. He was tragically killed in a T-38 training accident on 4 September 1970. Robert Herres also returned to the Flight Test School and eventually served as Vice Chairman of the Joint Chiefs of Staff. The MOL program had attracted uniquely talented and ambitious crew members. Even after the program was canceled, those crew members continued to serve their country and pursue impressive careers.

MOL's Termination and its Hardware

MOL had talented people to offer the community, and it also had hardware. During June and July, an ad hoc group, chaired by MOL technical director Michael Yarymovych, was organized to ensure maximum national benefit from MOL hardware, technology, and experience. The group reviewed all MOL hardware, facilities, and technology, and coordinated with both industry and NASA to find the best use for MOL residuals.[209] All crew-related equipment, as well as the Gemini, would be transferred to NASA. The SLC-6 launch facility was to be "mothballed" and kept in a "down-mode" for possible future use. In summary, "The review by the Ad Hoc Group revealed that a sizeable percentage of the engineering test hardware had been completed, and fabrication of flight articles had commenced. In this regard, an unmeasurable but real benefit of the program is the expansion of manned spaceflight know-how across a broad segment of industry and Government."[210]

Transferring assets to NASA was a long process, however. In October 1969, a joint Air Force and NASA review found that MOL's Acquisition and Tracking System (ATS), as well as the Mission Development Simulator (MDS), may have application to NASA, though GE would conduct a study to assess whether or not NASA could use it.[211] The inventory in question was significant, as the residual MOL hardware was estimated in value at $12.5 million.[212] By March 1970, NASA planned to take both MOL's ATS and MDS, transferring them both quietly and without a public release of information.[213] Although quiet, the transition was not simple. A full year after initial meetings, in October 1970, leadership was still discussing the fate of MOL hardware. Some argued that due to the security concerns surrounding MOL, any hardware not transferred to NASA needed to be destroyed.[214] Coordinating storage facilities and determining plans for the hardware slowed the process. But by June 1970, DNRO McLucas wrote to Homer Newell, Associate Administrator at NASA, hopeful the transfer would happen soon.[215] There were a number of MOL residuals to transfer, and more than two years later, in February 1973, NASA and the Air Force were still coordinating.[216] By the end of 1973, manned system components, as well as the Laboratory Module Simulator and Mission Simulator, were finally handed over to NASA.[217]

With personnel and hardware redistributed, MOL offices closed down. The MOL program office located in the Pentagon closed on 15 February 1970, and in his capacity as Director for the Secretary of the Air Force Space Systems, Brig. Gen. Lew Allen was named point of contact for all residual MOL activities.[218] The MOL System Office in Los Angeles was scheduled to close on 30 June 1970, but DNRO McLucas extended the deadline, and the office closed officially on 30 September 1970.[219] Even with program offices closed, there were a number of tasks requiring attention. In June 1973, three contracts – with Aerojet, McDonnell Douglas, and United Technology Corporation – remained open and three personnel – Tom Rutter from the Secretary of the Air Force Special Projects, Bob Best from SAMSO, and William Merrill with Air Force Logistics Command – were working to complete all unfinished business.[220] Although program termination happened quickly and abruptly for many, closing out all MOL-related tasks was a long and arduous process.

Looking Back and Lessons Learned

The MOL concept faced skepticism and criticism from the very beginning, though many believed deeply in its potential. Reflecting on the program 45 years after its termination, Bob Crippen stated, "It sounded like a productive use of people [at the time], and I still believe that people in the military could provide benefits to the station….. I thought it was an important program, and I'm glad that they did finally declassify some information on it. I wish it had a little bit more publicity than what it did, but it was a good program."[221] Likewise, Macleay claimed, "I was convinced that if we ever got up there and showed what man could really do, there would be a lot of follow-on things to do. That wasn't going to be the end of the program… I was convinced."[222] Quietly and prematurely canceled, one can only speculate on what the program could have been. Truly stated, "I wish it had flown. I think it would have been an amazing capability."[223]

> *"I don't care how far along the program is, it can go away in a heartbeat."*

Although MOL never flew, those involved learned invaluable lessons. One hard lesson learned was that no program is safe. Crippen explained, "I don't care how far along the program is, it can go away in a heartbeat."[224] Abrahamson similarly stated, "All programs are in jeopardy all the time because there are many things the country needs that exceed the budget potential of the country. You have to find ways to explain what you're doing and why to the right people. And you have to show progress."[225] When asked about other lessons learned, Crippen explained, "[The program] really sort of taught me how to go out and interface with contractors… Also, I saw some examples of leadership that I thought were very good to be able to follow."[226] Abrahamson walked away with a greater appreciation for understanding the entirety of a program. He described, "The whole issue of understanding a program, not just from the viewpoint of what is the mission that the program manager gets handled, but you really have to understand how it's going to go all the way down to the user. That is so vital now. You're always adapting something for something else."[227]

The MOL program was designed to push boundaries – to gain needed intelligence and explore what man could do from space. While development faced major hurdles and the program was canceled before it ever had a chance to fly, MOL was a proving ground for young officers, and all walked away from the program better prepared for the future. Technology was transferred to other programs, and crew members, shaped by their experiences on MOL, applied their knowledge and experience to new programs. Although the program was canceled, the technology developed and lessons learned were invaluable. Dick Truly reflected fondly, "It was an amazing experience for a young officer."[228]

Endnotes

1. Letter, Albert C. Hall to Dr. Brown, 24 August 1965, Job 199900019-10-003C, NROARC.

2. Memorandum for Record, Sub: 8 November 1965 PSAC Reconnaissance Panel Roundtable Discussion on DORIAN, 10 November 1965, Job 199700076-02-005-013, NROARC.

3. Reconnaissance Panel Views on the MOL Development Program, 18 November 1965, Job 199700063-04-016-031, NROARC.

4. Ibid.

5. Ibid.

6. Memorandum, McMillan to Martin, 29 September 1965, Job 199700063-04-016-034, NROARC.

7. DIAMOND II Study, Job 199800074-05-111, NROARC.

8. Ibid.

9. Memorandum, Schriever to Secretary of the Air Force, Sub: MOL Monthly Status Report for December, 4 January 1966, Job 199700033-08-026A, NROARC.

10. Ibid.

11. Ibid.

12. Memorandum, Charlie at Executive Office of the President, Bureau of the Budget to McNamara, 21 March 1966, Job 199700057-01-002-018, NROARC.

13. Memorandum, Worthman to Flax, Sub: PSAC Panel Comments on the MOL, 19 August 1966, Job 199700063-04-016-025, NROARC.

14. Ibid.

15. Memorandum for Record, Yarymovych (MOL Technical Director), Sub: PSAC Review of MOL Program, 5 September 1967, NROARC.

16. Ibid.

17. Contributions of Man in the MOL/DORIAN System, prepared by Aerospace and signed by Harry Bernstein (Associate Group Director, Operations Directorate, MOL), October 1967, Job 199900021-04-024, NROARC.

18. Ibid.

19. Memorandum, Stewart and Ferguson to Secretary of the Air Force, Sub: MOL Monthly Status Report for August, 7 September 1967, Job 199700033-08-028C, NROARC.

20. Development Problems Inherent in an Unmanned Dorian System, 1966, Job 199700063-04-016-020, NROARC.

21. Ibid.

22. Memorandum, Flax to Director of MOL, Sub: Policy Relating to MOL Astronauts, 28 December 1966, Job 199700050-02-008-015, NROARC.

23. Oral History Interview with Albert Crews, 24 March 2014, p. 4, CSNR/RC.

24. Comments on TWX on Provisions of DRV and WRDL in MOL, undated, Job 199700063-04-016-006, NROARC.

25. Memorandum for Record, Yarymovych, Sub: Manned Versus Unmanned MOL Cost Comparisons, 19 May 1967, Job 199700057-04-003-002, NROARC.

26. Ibid.

27. Ibid.

28. Ibid.

29. Memorandum, Evans to Flax, Sub: Contingency Planning for MOL flights 5, 6, and 7, 9 November 1966, Job 199700063-01-010-001, NROARC.

30   Memorandum, Colonel Walter W. Sanders to Stewart, Sub: Convertibility in the MOL Program, 27 April 1967, Job 199700057-03-008-002, NROARC.

31   Convertibility in the MOL Program report, MOL Program Office, 27 April 1967, Job 199700057-03-008-003, NROARC.

32   Ibid.

33   Memorandum, H. Barfield to Foster, Sub: Questions on MOL, 13 June 1967, NROARC.

34   Ibid.

35   Ibid.

36   Memorandum for the Director Defense Research and Engineering, Sub: Comparison of MOL to an Unmanned System, Job 199700063-04-019-004, NROARC.

37   Memorandum, Brown to Secretary of Defense, Sub: MOL program, 15 December 1967, Job 199700076-02-007-019, NROARC.

38   Memorandum for Record, Colonel Ralph Ford (Chief, Program and Policies Division, SAFSL), Sub: MOL/DORIAN Briefing to House Committee on Science and Astronautics Members, 8 February 1968, Job 199700037-03-016-001, NROARC.

39   Memorandum, Department of State to Secretary of the Air Force, Sub: An Offer of Inspection of the MOL, 8 October 1965, Job 199700063-04-002-004, NROARC.

40   Ibid.

41   Ibid.

42   Ibid.

43   Memorandum, Brown to Assistant Secretary of Defense for International Security Affairs, Sub: Review – an Offer of Inspection of MOL, 15 October 1965, Job 199700063-04-002-022, NROARC.

44   Ibid.

45   Memorandum, Alvin Friedman to Brown, Sub: MOL Inspection Proposal, 23 October 1965, Job 199700063-04-002-030, NROARC.

46   Ibid.

47   ENDC Meeting Contingency Paper, Sub: Soviet Orbital Rockets and the U.S. MOL, 27 January 1966, Job 199700066-04-012-045, NROARC.

48   Ibid.

49   Ibid.

50   Memorandum, Paul Goulder (Assistant Secretary of Defense) to Flax, Sub: Release of Technical Papers on MOL, 10 June 1968, Job 199700049-05-001-036, NROARC.

51   Ibid.

52   High Resolution Photography Volume I – Text, 15 January 1968 (revised from 20 October 1967), Job 199900021-02-001D, NROARC.

53   Letter, Stewart to Flax, Sub: MOL/DORIAN Reconnaissance System briefing, 23 September 1966, Job 199700063-04-016-023, NROARC.

54   MOL/DORIAN Program working material, H. Bernstein, 24 July 1967, Job 199900021-04-006B, NROARC.

55   Memorandum, Stewart to Flax, 31 July 1967, Job 199700070-02-024-039, NROARC.

56   Memorandum for Record, Stewart, Sub: PRC Meeting, 19 March 1968, Job 199700066-05-007, NROARC.

57   Ibid.

58   Memorandum, Sub: The Intelligence Value of the MOL Program, 15 May 1968, Job 199700070-02-18-019, NROARC.

59   Ibid.

60 The Value of Very High Resolution Photography – Volume I, Manned Orbiting Laboratory Program Office, 15 August 1968, Job 199700058-01-021A, NROARC.

61 Ibid.

62 The Need for Very High Resolution Imagery and its Contribution to DOD Operations and Decisions: Volume I – Executive Summary, November 1968, Job 199700057-05-001, NROARC.

63 Ibid.

64 Memorandum, Major Richard Greer to Captain Geiger, Sub: Rationalization of VHR, 15 September 1969, Job 199800073-01-039, NROARC.

65 Memorandum, Ivan Selin (Deputy Assistant Secretary of Defense) to Deputy Secretary of Defense, Sub: Comments on the MOL Development Paper and the DDR&E/DIA Study of Very High Resolution (VHR) Imagery, 24 January 1969, Job 199700070-03-010-001, NROARC.

66 Ibid.

67 Memorandum, Foster to Deputy Secretary of Defense, Sub: MOL Program and VHR Imagery, 31 January 1969, Job 199700070-03-010-006, NROARC.

68 Oral History Interview with James Abrahamson, 20 June 2013, p. 6, CSNR/RC.

69 Ibid, p. 10.

70 Report, Complimentary Apollo Applications and MOL Program, 24 October 1967, Job 199800058-01-140, NROARC.

71 Ibid.

72 Ibid.

73 Talking Paper, MOL/AAP Considerations, November 1967, Job 199700073-03-014-001, NROARC.

74 Ibid.

75 Memorandum, Foster to Deputy Secretary of Defense, Sub: DOD/NASA Joint Program Review, 27 June 1968, Job 199700046-03-012-007, NROARC.

76 Ibid.

77 Memorandum, Bleymaier to Stewart, Sub: MOL Monthly management Report for 26 September – 25 October 1968, 14 November 1968, Job 199700033-09-013-002, NROARC.

78 Oral History Interview with Robert Crippen, 24 March 2014, p. 5, CSNR/RC.

79 Oral History Interview with Richard Truly, 4 June 2014, p. 10, CSNR/RC.

80 Memorandum, Schriever to Secretary of the Air Force, Sub: MOL Monthly Status Report for November 1965, 9 December 1965, Job 199700033-08-024-001, NROARC.

81 Ibid.

82 Memorandum, Evans and Ferguson to Secretary of the Air Force, Sub: MOL Monthly Status Report for February, 6 March 1967, Job 199700033-08-027E, NROARC.

83 MOL Monthly Progress Reports for 1 July 1968 through 31 July 1968, J.F. Chalmers (Director, Management Systems and Administration, Manned Orbiting Laboratory Division, System Engineering Operations), undated, Job 199900021-02-047, NROARC.

84 Letter, Aerospace Corporation (Walter C Williams, Vice President, General Manager, MOL Division) to MOL Systems Office (Bleymaier), Sub: Manpower, 25 November 1968, Job 199900021-07-005, NROARC.

85 Memorandum, Colonel Ralph Ford (Chief, Program and Policies Division, SAFSL) to Mr. Palley, Sub: MOL Development Costs, 27 August 1968, Job 199700049-05-002-005, NROARC.

86 Memorandum, John Kirk (Special Assistant, Southeast Asia Matters) to Foster, Sub: Past Experience on the MOL Program, 22 November 1968, Job 199700070-03-009-028, NROARC.

87 Letter, Helms to Paul Nitze (Deputy Secretary of Defense), 6 December 1968, Job 199700070-02-018-032, NROARC.

88   MOL, 14 April 1969, Job 199700070-02-005-002, NROARC.

89   Ibid.

90   Memorandum for Record, Stewart, Sub: MOL Policy Committee Meeting of 9 May 1969, undated, Job 199700033-07-04, NROARC.

91   Memorandum, Foster to Secretary of Defense, Sub: MOL Program Funding, 14 April 1969, Job 199700070-03-010-012, NROARC.

92   Ibid.

93   MOL Program Chronology, undated, Job 199700057-04-002-009, NROARC.

94   Oral History Interview with Lachlan Macleay, 2 June 2014, p. 13, CSNR/RC.

95   Oral History Interview with Karol Bobko, 3 April 2014, p. 5, CSNR/RC.

96   Oral History Interview with Robert Crippen, 24 March 2014, p. 5, CSNR/RC.

97   Minutes of Meeting 66-2, Air Force MOL Policy Committee, 29 April 1966, Job 199700033-09-016-009, NROARC.

98   Memorandum for Record, Sub: March 10 Meeting on MOL Revised Costs/Schedules, 14 March 1967, Job 199700033-07-053, NROARC.

99   Memorandum, Stewart and Ferguson to Secretary of the Air Force, Sub: MOL Monthly Status Report for March, 5 April 1967, Job 199700033-08-027F, NROARC.

100   Memorandum for Record, Sub: Minutes, 14 April 1967 MOL Management Meeting, Job 199700033-07-053, NROARC.

101   Memorandum for Record, Stewart, Sub: Minutes, 11 May 1967 MOL Management Meeting, Job 199700066-05-023A, NROARC.

102   Program Chronology, undated, Job 199700057-04-002-009, NROARC.

103   Memorandum, Stewart and Ferguson to Secretary of the Air Force, Sub: MOL Monthly Status Report for October, 7 November 1967, Job 199700033-08-028E, NROARC.

104   Memorandum for Record, Stewart, Sub: Minutes, November 17 MOL Program Review Committee Meeting, 17 November 1967, Job 199700066-05-001, NROARC.

105   Memorandum, Ferguson to Secretary of the Air Force, Sub: MOL Monthly Status Report through 30 November 1967, 6 December 1967, Job 199700033-08-028BB, NROARC.

106   Memorandum, Stewart to Flax, Sub: Deferral of Development of the Unmanned MOL System, 1 June 1968, Job 19700057-04-002-006, NROARC.

107   Trip Report, Bertram Kemp, Sub: Air Force/Contractor MOL Program Rescheduling Meeting, 22 July, Job 199700057-04-002-003, NROARC.

108   Oral History Interview with Albert Crews, 24 March 2014, p. 4, CSNR/RC.

109   Oral History Interview with Lachlan Macleay, 2 June 2014, p. 12, CSNR/RC.

110   Oral History Interview with Richard Truly, 4 June 2014, p. 9, CSNR/RC.

111   Oral History Interview with Albert Crews, 24 March 2014, p. 4, CSNR/RC.

112   Memorandum, Stewart and Ferguson to Secretary of the Air Force, Sub: MOL Monthly Status Report for August, 9 September 1968, Job 199700033-08-029D, NROARC.

113   Oral History Interview with James Abrahamson, 20 June 2013, p. 10, CSNR/RC.

114   Paper, Reliability Growth and Cost Effectiveness Comparison of Manned and Unmanned MOL Systems, 16 May 1966, Job 199700063-03-004-007, NROARC.

115   Paper, Basis for Confidence in Achieving the Objectives of MOL, C. P. Spoelhof, 8 September 1967, Job 199700063-04-016-001, NROARC.

116 Memorandum, Yarymovych to Stewart, Sub: Response to Secretary of Defense on MOL Program, 13 December 1967, Job 199700050-02-011-014, NROARC.

117 Ibid.

118 Oral History Interview with Lachlan Macleay, 2 June 2014, p. 13, CSNR/RC.

119 MOL Backup Material for Congressional Hearings, 1969, Job 199700076-02-009-001, NROARC.

120 Ibid.

121 Memorandum for Record, Worthman, Sub: The Rivers Committee and MOL, 28 May 1969, Job 199700070-03-011-005, NROARC.

122 Ibid.

123 Paper, Sub: MOL briefing Policy, Job 199700033-01-046-002, NROARC.

124 Ibid.

125 Oral History Interview with James Abrahamson, 20 June 2013, p. 15, CSNR/RC.

126 Draft, Allen, Sub: MOL, 18 February 1969, Job 199700070-03-010-006, NROARC.

127 Ibid.

128 Paper, Mission Value, Manned Orbiting Laboratory Program, 28 March 1969, Job 199700058-01-021B, NROARC.

129 Memorandum for Record, Ford, Sub: Briefing to Dr. McLucas, 15 April 1969, Job 199700033-07-002, NROARC.

130 Memorandum, Stewart and Ferguson to Secretary of the Air Force, Sub: MOL Monthly Status Report for December, 13 January 1969, Job 199700033-08-031B, NROARC.

131 MOL Monthly Progress Report for 1 February thru 28 February 1969, J. F. Chalmers (Systems Engineering Director, Management Systems) and W. C. Williams (Vice President, General Manager, MOL division), 19 March 1969, Job 199900021-02-054, NROARC.

132 Ibid.

133 Memorandum, R. H. Campbell (SAFSLO), Sub: Intelligence Targets for MOL Crew Training, 4 February 1969, Job 199700070-02-019-003, NROARC.

134 Covering Brief, Stewart to Flax, 1 June 1968, Job 199700076-02-007-022, NROARC.

135 Development Concept Paper, DDR&E Office, Sub: MOL, 4 December 1968, Job 199700076-02-008-008, NROARC.

136 Memorandum, Nevin Palley (Asst Director – Space Technology) to DDR&E, Sub: MOL Program Alternative Decision, 10 March 1969, Job 199700076-02-008-011, NROARC.

137 BYEMAN message, Stewart to Bleymaier, 1 April 1969, Job 199700070-02-019-002, NROARC.

138 Memorandum, Foster to Secretary of Defense and Deputy Secretary of Defense, Sub: PSAC Review of MOL, 25 April 1969, Job 199700070-03-010-017, NROARC.

139 Ibid.

140 Briefing Charts, Sub: MOL Status Report, MOL Policy Committee Meeting, 9 May 1969, Job 199700033-07-04, NROARC.

141 Ibid.

142 Ibid.

143 Memorandum for Record, Stewart, Sub: MOL Policy Committee Meeting of 9 May 1969, undated, Job 199700033-07-04, NROARC.

144 Memorandum, Mayo to Packard, 13 February 1969, Job 199700057-04-002-001, NROARC.

145 Memorandum to Deputy Secretary of Defense, Sub: Budget issues on MOL, Hexagon and Drones, 19 February 1969, Job 199700057-04-001-009, NROARC.

146   Ibid.

147   Ibid.

148   Ibid.

149   Memorandum, Seamans to Deputy Secretary of Defense, Sub: MOL Program Alternatives, 26 February 1969, Job 199700057-04-001-009, NROARC.

150   Ibid.

151   Memorandum, Stewart to Seamans, Sub: MOL funding, 26 March 1969, Job 199700057-04-001-007, NROARC.

152   Ibid.

153   Memorandum, Stewart to Seamans, Sub: MOL FY 70 Program Options, 22 April 1969, Job 199700057-04-001-003, NROARC.

154   Ibid.

155   Letter, Stewart to Ferguson, 28 April 1969, NROARC.

156   Memorandum, Seamans to Deputy Secretary of Defense, Sub: MOL FY 70 Program Options, 30 April 1969, Job 199700057-04-001-004, NROARC.

157   Ibid.

158   Memorandum for Record, Stewart, Sub: MOL Policy Committee Meeting of 9 May 1969, undated, Job 199700033-07-04, NROARC.

159   Oral History Interview with Robert Crippen, 24 March 2014, p. 8, CSNR/RC.

160   Memorandum for Record, Stewart, Sub: Meeting with the President re: MOL, 19 May 1969, Job 199700076-02-009-005, NROARC.

161   Ibid.

162   Ibid.

163   Paper, rough copy of MOL/STG paper, 6 June 1969, Job 199900021-02-058, NROARC.

164   Ibid.

165   Ibid.

166   Ibid.

167   Memorandum, Foster and Seaman (Department of Air Force) to Secretary of Defense, Sub: MOL Decision, 6 June 1969, Job 199700066-05-005-003, NROARC.

168   Ibid.

169   Ibid.

170   Letter, Colonel John Shaugnessy (Chief, Plans Group, Legislative Liaison), 10 June 1969, Job 199700070-03-011-006, NROARC.

171   Memorandum for Basic Message Center, Stewart to Bleymaier, 7 June 1969, Job 199700066-05-005-001, NROARC.

172   Ibid.

173   Ibid.

174   Ibid.

175   Paper, MOL Program Background, 8 June 1969, Job 199700066-05-005-002, NROARC.

176   Ibid.

177   Memorandum to Secretary of the Air Force, Director, National Reconnaissance Office, 9 June 1969, Job 199700066-05-005-007, NROARC.

178 Oral History Interview with Karol Bobko, 3 April 2014, p. 8, CSNR/RC.

179 Ibid, p. 11.

180 Oral History Interview with Robert Crippen, 24 March 2014, p. 7, CSNR/RC.

181 Oral History Interview with Lachlan Macleay, 2 June 2014, p. 15, CSNR/RC.

182 Oral History Interview with James Abrahamson, 20 June 2013, p. 15, CSNR/RC.

183 Oral History Interview with Lachlan Macleay, 2 June 2014, p. 15, CSNR/RC.

184 Oral History Interview with Richard Truly, 4 June 2014, p. 13, CSNR/RC.

185 Ibid, p. 14.

186 Oral History Interview with Lachlan Macleay, 2 June 2014, p. 16, CSNR/RC.

187 Oral History Interview with Albert Crews, 24 March 2014, p. 7, CSNR/RC.

188 Ibid, p. 11.

189 Oral History Interview with Robert Crippen, 24 March 2014, p. 8, CSNR/RC.

190 Oral History Interview with Lachlan Macleay, 2 June 2014, p. 18, CSNR/RC.

191 Memorandum, G.D. McGhee to B.F. Knolle, Sub: Technical Status of the Dorian Payload at the Time of Termination, 27 June 1969, Job 199900021-05-012, NROARC.

192 Oral History Interview with Robert Crippen, 24 March 2014, p. 5, CSNR/RC.

193 Oral History Interview with Richard Truly, 4 June 2014, p. 7-8, CSNR/RC.

194 Ibid, p. 9

195 Memorandum, Ferguson to Seamans and McLucas, Sub: MOL Program Close-Out Status, 23 December 1969, Job 199700066-05-005-039, NROARC.

196 Memorandum, Stewart to Seamans, Sub: MOL Termination Status Report, 3 July 1969, Job 199700066-05-005-021, NROARC.

197 Memorandum, Ferguson to Seamans and McLucas, Sub: MOL Program Close-Out Status, 23 December 1969, Job 199700066-05-005-039, NROARC.

198 Memorandum, Bleymaier to Ferguson and McLucas, Sub: MOL Systems Office Post Termination Report, undated, Job 199700066-05-004, NROARC.

199 Oral History Interview with Robert Crippen, 24 March 2014, p. 9, CSNR/RC.

200 Ibid.

201 Oral History Interview with Richard Truly, 4 June 2014, p. 14, CSNR/RC.

202 Oral History Interview with Robert Crippen, 24 March 2014, p. 9, CSNR/RC.

203 Oral History Interview with Karol Bobko, 3 April 2014, p. 9, CSNR/RC.

204 Oral History Interview with Lachlan Macleay, 2 June 2014, p. 17, CSNR/RC.

205 Oral History Interview with Albert Crews, 24 March 2014, p. 4-5, CSNR/RC.

206 Ibid, p. 8.

207 Oral History Interview with Lachlan Macleay, 2 June 2014, p. 17, CSNR/RC.

208 Oral History Interview with James Abrahamson, 20 June 2013, p. 9, CSNR/RC.

209 Review of MOL Residuals, Ad Hoc Group (approved by Chairman Yarymovych), 1 August 1969, Job 199700070-03-012-001, NROARC.

210 Ibid.

211 Statement of Work, 31 October 1969, Job 199700073-03-001-003, NROARC.

212 Letter, McLucas to Homer Newell, 4 February 1970, Job 199700073-01-010-018, NROARC.

213 Letter, Homer Newell to McLucas, 30 March 1970, 199700070-04-012-009, NROARC.

214 Talking Paper for Meeting with General Smart, 1 October 1970, Job 199700070-04-012-032, NROARC.

215 Letter, McLucas to Newell, 16 June 1970, 199700066-01-011-015, NROARC.

216 Memorandum for Record, Frederick Hofmann, Sub: MOL Residuals at Item, 1 February 1973, Job 199700073-03-008-015, NROARC.

217 Note, Frederick Hofmann to Yarymovych, Sub: MOL Residuals Transferred to NASA, 15 October 1973, Job 199700073-03-009-010, NROARC.

218 Memorandum, to All OSAF Offices (AFCCS), Sub: MOL Program, 8 January 1970, Job 199800074-05-094, NROARC.

219 Memorandum for Record, Fredrick Hofmann, Sub: MOL Program Office Close Out, 18 September 1970, Job 199700066-01-010-020, NROARC.

220 Memorandum, Norbert Malecka to Mr. Holleran, Sub: MOL status, 5 June 1973, Job 200800131-01-009, NROARC.

221 Oral History Interview with Robert Crippen, 24 March 2014, p. 3-10, CSNR/RC.

222 Oral History Interview with Lachlan Macleay, 2 June 2014, p. 20, CSNR/RC.

223 Oral History Interview with Richard Truly, 4 June 2014, p. 16, CSNR/RC.

224 Oral History Interview with Robert Crippen, 24 March 2014, p. 10, CSNR/RC.

225 Oral History Interview with James Abrahamson, 20 June 2013, p. 16, CSNR/RC.

226 Oral History Interview with Robert Crippen, 24 March 2014, p. 10, CSNR/RC.

227 Oral History Interview with James Abrahamson, 20 June 2013, p. 17-18, CSNR/RC.

228 Oral History Interview with Richard Truly, 4 June 2014, p. 15, CSNR/RC.

INDEX

A

Abrahamson, James A. 30, 38, 39, 41, 46, 52, 55, 56, 57, 58, 61, 62, 75, 80, 81, 88, 92, 93, 94
Adams, Michael J. 31, 35, 79, 90
Aerojet 93
Aerospace Corporation 12, 21, 46, 77
Allen, Lew, Jr. 81, 93
Apollo 4, 58, 61, 69, 75, 76, 77, 85

B

Berg, Russell A. 14, 21, 31
Bernstein, Harry 74
Best, Robert 93
Bleymaier, Joseph S. 16, 23, 55, 82, 84, 87
Block, Eddie 58
Bobko, Karol J. 35, 36, 37, 45, 46, 48, 49, 51, 52, 53, 54, 55, 57, 59, 60, 61, 78, 88, 90, 91
Boeing Company 5, 21
Brady, William 5
Brooks Air Force Base 29
Brown, Harold 5, 7, 15, 22, 70, 72, 73, 78, 85
Buchanan, Buck 23
Bundy, McGeorge 9

C

Carroll, James 74
Casey, Walt 89
Corona 7
Crews, Albert H. Jr. 3, 30, 31, 32, 35, 46, 47, 48, 49, 55, 59, 61, 71, 79, 89, 92
Crippen, Robert L. 17, 23, 35, 36, 37, 41, 45, 46, 47, 54, 59, 76, 78, 86, 88, 89, 90, 91, 92, 93

D

Dietrich, Fred 90
Dorian 15, 17, 70, 74, 90
Douglas Aircraft Company 3, 5, 21, 46, 47
DynaSoar 1, 2, 3, 32

E

Easter Island 19
Eastman Kodak Company 4, 21, 59, 78, 79, 90
Eighteen Nation Disarmament Committee 73
Evans, Harry L. 8, 13, 14, 16, 21, 35, 72

F

Ferguson, James 22, 79, 84, 86
Finley, John L. 29, 30, 31, 33, 34, 57, 79, 90
Flax, Alexander H. 7, 15, 19, 59, 61, 62, 71, 78, 79, 83, 85
Foster, John S., Jr. 15, 62, 75, 76, 78, 83, 85, 87
Friedman, Alvin 73
Fullerton, C. Gordon 36, 37, 91
Funk, Ben I. 16

G

Gambit 7, 51
Gemini B 4, 11, 16, 19, 20, 47, 60
General Electric Company 3, 5, 21, 47, 55
Glass, Larry 11
Goulder, Paul 73
Greer, Robert E. 4

H

Hall, Albert C. 6
Hall, W. C. 6
Hamilton Standard 21
Hartsfield, Henry W., Jr. 34, 36, 37, 41, 57, 91
Helms, Richard 51, 74, 77
Hermann, Robert 38
Herres, Robert T. 38, 40, 41, 58, 91, 92
Hornig, Donald F. 8, 69, 70
Humphrey, Hubert 51

J

Johnson, Lyndon B. 3, 13, 14, 76

K

Keeling, Gerald F. 22
Keeny, Spurgeon M., Jr. 9
Kemp, Bertram 79
Kirk, John 77
Kissinger, Henry 86
Kitchen, Jeffrey C. 9

L

Laboratory Module 16, 17, 18
Laird, Melvin R. 86, 87, 89
Land, Edwin H. 69, 70, 71
Lawrence, Robert H., Jr. 38, 40, 90
Lawyer, Richard E. 31, 33, 47, 55, 57
Lawyer, Richard H. 92
Lockheed Corporation 5, 21

M

Macleay, Lachlan 19, 23, 29, 30, 31, 33, 34, 38, 41, 46, 49, 51 - 53, 55 - 57, 76, 78 - 80, 88, 89, 90, 92, 93
Martin, John L., Jr. 4, 15, 16, 22, 23, 79
Martin Marietta Corporation 4, 12, 21, 58
Mathews, Charles W. 61
Mayo, Robert 84, 86
Mazza, Louis F. 8, 9, 46
McDonnell Aircraft Corporation 4, 12, 21, 46, 60
McDonnell Douglas 93
McLucas, John L. 82, 88, 93
McMillan, Brockway 4, 6, 13, 15, 70
McNamara, Robert 2, 3, 5, 10, 11, 13, 21, 60, 70
McNaughton, John T. 9
Merrill, William 93
Miller, George 91
Mission Payload System Segment 16

N

NASA 2, 10, 13, 35, 55, 56, 58, 60, 61, 75, 76, 89 - 92
National Photographic Interpretation Center 58
Neubeck, Francis G. 31, 34, 58, 92
Newell, Homer 93
Nixon, Richard M. 78, 81, 86
North American Aviation 4

O

Overmyer, Robert F. 36, 38, 47, 55, 91

P

Packard, David 84, 87, 88
Peterson, Donald H. 38, 41, 58, 91
Purcell, Edward M. 70

R

Raborn, William 10
Resolution 7, 8, 10, 11 - 14, 16, 19, 45, 46, 49, 51, 53, 61, 62, 70 - 75, 80, 81, 84, 85, 87
Rusk, Dean 10
Rutter, Thomas 90, 93

S

Santa Fe and Stolte 61
Schlesinger, James R. 86
Schriever, Bernard Adolph 3, 7, 13, 14, 15, 16, 22, 30, 45, 61
Seaborg, Glenn 10
Seamans, Robert C., Jr. 85, 86, 87, 88
Selin, Ivan 75
Shaughnessy, John 87
Skantze, Larry 23, 41, 87
Slayton, Deke 90, 92
SLC-6 61, 83, 88, 92
Soviet Union 1, 2, 10, 19, 58, 59, 73, 77
Space Target 62
Stashevski, G.S. 58
Steininger, Donald H. 70
Stewart, James T. 8, 61, 74, 78, 79, 83, 84, 85, 86, 87
Sylvester, Arthur 59

T

Taylor, James M. 31, 34, 58, 92
Titan III 2, 11, 17, 20, 21
Truly, Richard
Truly, Richard H. 19, 21, 29 - 31, 34, 41, 46, 47, 49, 51 - 54, 56 - 58, 61, 76, 79, 88 - 94
TRW Inc. 90

U

United Technology Center 12
United Technology Corporation 93

V

Vandenberg Air Force Base 11, 17, 83, 88
Very High Resolution Photography 7, 10, 19, 62, 74, 75, 81

W

Webb, James 10, 60
Williams, Walter C. 77
Worthman, Paul E. 10, 13, 16

Y

Yarymovych, Michael I. 71, 80, 92
Yeager, Chuck 29, 30

Z

Zuckert, Eugene M. 3, 15

www.ingramcontent.com/pod-product-compliance
Lightning Source LLC
Chambersburg PA
CBHW080548170426
43195CB00016B/2716